THE HEART CONDITION

NATHANYAEL O. WEST

LifeRich Publishing is a registered trademark of The Reader's Digest Association, Inc.

LifeRich Publishing books may be ordered through booksellers or by contacting:

LifeRich Publishing
1663 Liberty Drive
Bloomington, IN 47403
www.liferichpublishing.com
1 (888) 238-8637

Because of the dynamic nature of the Internet, any web addresses or links contained in
this book may have changed since publication and may no longer be valid. The views
expressed in this work are solely those of the author and do not necessarily reflect the
views of the publisher, and the publisher hereby disclaims any responsibility for them.

Any people depicted in stock imagery provided by Thinkstock are models,
and such images are being used for illustrative purposes only.
Certain stock imagery © Thinkstock.

ISBN: 978-1-4897-0499-3 (sc)
ISBN: 978-1-4897-0500-6 (hc)
ISBN: 978-1-4897-0501-3 (e)

Library of Congress Control Number: 2015947980

Print information available on the last page.

LifeRich Publishing rev. date: 12/23/2015

Through patience a ruler is persuaded; and a gentle word can break a bone.

-Proverbs 25:15

CONTENTS

ACKNOWLEDGEMENTS

To my mother, Carole West– the first instance I knew of love, and to my late father: George West, who taught me the art of tenacity and resilience in an unforgiving and sometimes inhospitable world. I love you both.

To my friends, to my family, and most importantly to God –the author and finisher of my faith. Thank you for allowing me to be your writing partner.

This book is dedicated to individuals like (and including) myself: truth seekers, who in honest reflection are willing to stop, hold the inner workings of their heart up to *The Light*, and acknowledge that the subsequently cast shadows only pinpoint and expose the obstructions, which we ourselves have placed before God.

I celebrate you for being discerning in your choice - to pursue, with a receptive heart and a sound mind, a deeper level of relationship with The Creator of All Things. Your walk is mine.

#iProfessJesus

INTRODUCTION

Thank you for taking the opportunity to invest in your walk with God.

This is essentially a study aid, and so please treat it as such. Clear some time in your schedule, and sit down to read it with a dictionary and a Bible at hand to clarify any of the more ambiguous aspects of the language used in this book, or to contextualize what is being said. This is important for your own understanding, and subsequent assimilation.

Although this book is rich in revelation, please do not get caught up in the wonder, and miss the actual message. The Bible says that it is a wicked and adulterous generation which pursues after a sign [Matt. 16:4], with no concern for sound doctrine [2 Tim. 4:3]. In writing this book, as the revelation came, this is something God had to continually reinforce to my heart. Do not get so caught up in the forest, that you do not see the trees – even taking time to appreciate the leaves, the branches; and most importantly, to examine the fruit.

Finally, in love, this book is not a Bible, and is no substitute for The Word of God. Without The Bible this is a good read, at best. Only The Word of God has the ability to miraculously transform from within. I would therefore again encourage you to read this book alongside your Bible, as to verify its contents, and enable the correct application of its themes. This book may plant, your pastor may water, but it is God Himself who brings the increase.

I pray that this book and the words within are the catalyst for real transformational change, for the good, in your life and to your individual circumstances.

CHAPTER 1

THE HEART CONDITION: 101

⁹ In this was manifested the love of God toward us, because that God
sent his only begotten Son into the world, that we might live through
him. ¹⁰ Herein is love, not that we loved God, but that he loved us,
and sent his Son to be the [complete] propitiation for our sins. ¹¹
Beloved, if God so loved us, we ought also to love one another.

1 John 4:9-11
[KJV]

PROLOGUE

Beginning this chapter with the sentiment of the above scripture;
God loves us, so incredibly, and in the most incomprehensibly
whole sense of the word. In love, Jesus endured Calvary for you;
individually, intimately and <u>completely</u>; and because of Calvary,
EVERYTHING changes. Though the burden of this debt is great,
Jesus has wiped it – instead He invites us, <u>in love</u>, to become
enshrouded in the unadulterated decadence, sweetness and purity
of His love, to pursue *relationship*, and to become a partaker of the
perfect peace which abounds therein. When God looked at the state
of the world, considered the debauchery, wickedness and darkness
upon her face; when He saw the enemy's iron grip on His children; in

deciding to launch an attack, He did not send Michael; but trading majesty for mortality and glory for flesh, He sent Jesus - for the greatest of these is love [1 Cor. 13:13]. Essentially, love is the message of this book, attempting to awaken and (re)kindle that realization, where in love, the burning, insatiable appetite of <u>every</u> sub-atomic element of your being, every fiber, pulse and every sinew, <u>yields only</u> to the **truth** and **reality** of the one you love. *Selah.* It is in this place that we can truly begin to <u>stand</u> as sons and daughters, and articulate God's relentless love, in understanding, effectually and with absolute authority to the hearts of men.

God has declared the dwelling place of His choosing, '<u>Heaven</u>' – that is to say that although God is everywhere, simultaneously, He has chosen anchor Himself to a habitation (<u>Heaven</u>), and so whenever we see the purposed, tangible, heavy and deliberate presence or '*Kabod*' of God in a specific locality, we also witness the phenomena of '<u>Heaven</u>'. A very crude way of thinking about the '<u>Heaven</u>' phenomena, is akin to an individual with a distinctive signature fragrance – anyone in this individuals vicinity, will experience the fragrance, whist they experience the individual. The individual has chosen to make 'fragrance x' his signature fragrance, and so now, the two become almost synonymous. In Luke 17:21, Jesus said that The Kingdom of <u>Heaven</u> is within us. There is literally a designated place within your being, purposed to receive the '*Kabod*' of God - The heart. This *"Kabod"* is only experienced in "<u>Heaven</u>", and so IF the *Kabod* dwells in the heart of man; IF you have truly enthroned the King of Glory in your heart, then understand that the heart of man in which the Kabod dwells, is in fact by definition; *a type of* <u>Heaven</u>.

This is why it is so vital to allow God in, fully, so that *Heaven* can be ordered in and of our hearts. Out of the fullness, depth and abundance of the heart, the mouth speaks [Luke 6:45, Matthew 12:34]. Because of this, we – The Kingdom of God, through the lifestyle of compassion, are able, and dutifully expected to establish or 'plant *Heaven*' *[Isaiah 51:16]*, God's will for humanity, upon this earth – you are not being expected to establish something which is not already within you. THIS is the heart condition we should, as Christians be manifesting.

Throughout this book, reference will be made to *The Heart Condition* (THC). THC is simply a way of describing a specific series of systemic dysfunctions, which labor the heart of man; subsequently undermining the plan and purpose of God for the life of an individual at any given time. THC is a practically innate malady, which silently (but not without manifestation) plagues the hearts, and therefore lives of individuals - even Christian individuals, worldwide. THC's effect is often miss-appropriated under the guise of one of its several manifestations or symptoms, but at its core, its intention remains sacrosanct. In the same way that a virus will enter into a system, whether human, animal, plant or computer, and reprogram cells, thus undermining any 'healthy' function with a highly inefficient, corrupted expression; THC in the child of God, will cause the will of God to be inefficiently manifested in the life of a believer.

Sometimes we need to look in the mirror, and stare our ugly in the face – what is out of place? What needs fixing? There is no place for complacency in a relationship – familiarity is no excuse for laziness. Ezekiel 23 is one such a mirror, which will expose and magnify our imperfections. If we cannot see any aspect of the inglorious, ungrateful prostitute, Oholibah within ourselves [Ezekiel 23:11-19], we have told a lie. No matter what you have been duped into believing, Jesus, God's grace, and His mercy are not valid reasons to let yourself go! There is no admission in acknowledging that "all have sinned and fallen short", which justifies apathy in becoming the image of Christ <u>in this lifetime</u>. The Father calls us, saying 'Be ye holy, for I AM holy', and we do this out of love for God; not obligation. SO MUCH has been extended toward us, and our desire should be, to reach such a profound realization of Him, that every fiber of our being, glows with thanks, and we effortlessly live out the selfless truth of Galatians 2:20, 'I live, yet not I, but Christ liveth in me'.

3

Relationship is all encompassing, and is fed and strengthened by purposeful inclusion of what is conducive to relationship, and the exclusion of what isn't. A relationship is a living, breathing, growing entity, and so the reality is – and this may sound like a very stupid thing to say in the first chapter of a book, but – there *is* no book (I do not consider The Bible to be just 'a book', but The Word of God), no opinion, and no external advice ultimately, which will give you a perfect relationship. The only way to perfect a relationship, is with understanding, faithfulness, TIME – there are no shortcuts; and most importantly, with love. *This* is nothing more than our reasonable service.

Individuals who have labored with their bare hands for an extended period of time, are often characterized by their thick skinned, rough and calloused palms. This is the result of a 'conditioning process', which would cause the deformation, relative to exposure, over time. The same hands, under a different, continuous protocol, would become supple, softened/ less resilient, and more yielding or 'conditioned' to their new environment/ regime. As you progress, page by page, it is my intense, prayerful desire that a cascade of critical assessment and inner diagnostic evaluation would take place, causing a 'line upon line and precept upon precept' de-conditioning, and <u>Holy Spirit led reconditioning of the heart</u>. Only then is our heart truly able to experience, and express, the love wherein <u>trust without fear</u> abounds. The love through which, temptation, is no temptation, and there is no such thing as an alternative, or desire for supplementation. The love which overflows our heart, lubricates our minds, and washes our steps with butter on the road of holiness.

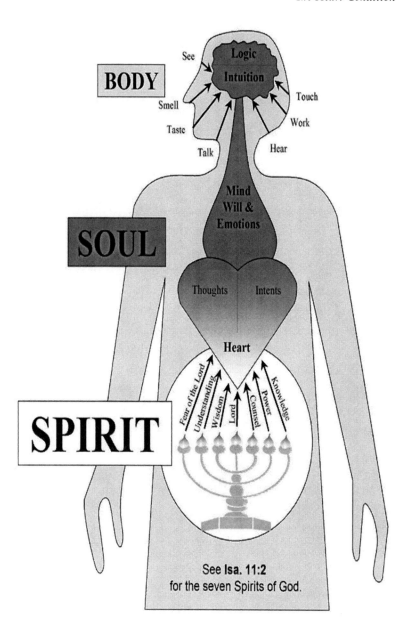

See **Isa. 11:2**
for the seven Spirits of God.

THE HEART

Thy word have I hid in mine heart, that I might not sin against thee.
Psalm 119:11
[AMP]

The (non-physical) heart is an amazing gift. As beautifully illustrated by the diagram on the previous page, the heart is a component of the whole man, and acts as a conduit between the spirit and the soul. In its composition, the heart is actually part soul - part spirit, and in a saved person the heart acts as a *type of Jesus*, in that it reconciles the spirit to the soul (which controls the flesh). In the same way that Jesus was made manifest in the flesh, bridging the gap between God and flesh; the heart being part sprit, part soul, is able to reconcile them. A heart under THC however, acts more like a type of Lucifer; cutting off the spirit, empowering the soul and spreading deception. Another understanding is that the heart modulates the soul, body and spirit, and therefore it is recognized that if the heart is not correctly aligned; it will be ineffective at modulation. In this, we can see that there may be many problematic manifestations in a person's life - symptoms, but the *root* of them all, lies with the modulator: the heart.

In the opening scripture, David writes that he has hidden The Word of God in his heart, to the effect that he would not sin against Him. Please don't confuse what I'm about to say for a new age philosophy. It is not - this is **Bible**, and holds information that we all need to understand; and in defining the heart, truly be equipped to identify its dysfunction, and move toward a more perfect representation of wholeness. The Bible says, 'as a man thinketh in his heart, so is he' [Proverbs 23:7], and truly, whatever we allow into our heart, is what will eventually end up manifesting into our life. This essentially speaks of the heart's nature as an <u>incubator</u> – this is why we talk about people '*harboring*' malice in their heart, for example. The heart has the innate capacity to bring whatever we are able to faithfully hold onto within it, whether fear; love; folly or good counsel, to maturity.

The Holy Spirit, The Word of God, and angel's, minister to the spirit. The spirit speaks to the heart. The *yielded* heart, gives instruction to the soul. The soul (the mind, the will and the emotions) influences the body, and the body manifests the ministered word. You can see how important the heart is, and how when the heart is out of order we would subsequently experience the manifestation of a 'strange' thing, at odds to what The Word of God says concerning our life. This is why David says he had *hidden* God's word in his heart, in the same way that a sower hides his seed in the ground. David knew that if he was able to keep the seed of The Word of God in his heart, that the harvest would come; he would reap righteousness, and therefore not sin against God. David's issue however, was that he planted a few more seeds in his ground, including the seed of his love for the female form, which manifested itself out of his heart into his soul, and who's harvest we read about in 2 Samuel 11-12. **In His choice for a King**, the young David was a man after God's own heart [Acts 13:22] – the heart of a shepherd, but as an adult, David was, at times, ineffectual in shepherding his own heart. David's Psalms are a telling collection of manuscripts which give us insight into how conflicted a man he was. David's love for God was unquestionable, *yet* in his heart, there was still prepared room for sin and folly.

> Keep *and* guard your heart with all vigilance *and* above
> all that you guard, for out of it flow the springs of life.
> **Proverbs 4:23**
> [AMP]

The functional heart is a closed system, one opening where it receives from the spirit, and one opening where it imparts to the soul. When Solomon wrote Proverbs 4:23, this is the order that he was talking about keeping and guarding. In THC, the heart is not effectively kept, and so the function is compromised – the spirit can no longer effectively influence the soul, or indeed, the soul can now influence the spirit, because the heart is no longer modulating as it should. This coupled with the fact that the heart is unguarded, and therefore can be ministered to by all manner external influences. This is very important. If you can identify a time in your life, where you have felt *deeply* discouraged by what you saw, heard, smelled tasted or felt, by what someone told you or by any other external instance, then you have identified a time past when your heart was unable to modulate trauma, and allowed it to influence the spirit. The majority of people will tell you that this is normal – we aren't robots, after all, and we have feelings. To this I would answer, no – we are not robots, and we have emotions yes, but over and above any emotion (which emanate from the soul), we have a spirit, which is ministered to by the Holy Spirit, and so there really is no excuse for anyone becoming disheartened (literally a disengaged heart), in Christ. As Lamentations puts it; 'Yet this I call to mind and therefore I have hope: Because of the LORD's great love we are not consumed, for his compassions never fail.'

<u>Wash away my sins</u>

In 1 Corinthians 10:13 [Amplified Translation], Paul recounts:

> For no temptation (no trial regarded as enticing to sin), [no matter how it comes or where it leads] has overtaken you and laid hold on you that is not common to man [that is, no temptation or trial has come to you that is beyond human resistance and that is not adjusted and adapted and belonging to human experience, and such as man can bear]. But God is faithful [to His Word and to His compassionate nature], and He [can be trusted] not to let you be tempted and tried and assayed beyond your ability and strength of resistance and power to endure, but with the temptation He will [always] also provide the way out (the means of escape to a landing place), that you may be capable and strong and powerful to bear up under it patiently.

This is interesting because the heart is an instrument which consistently provides exactly this – a way of escape, yet in popular culture, literature and philosophy, the heart is usually blamed when people find themselves in folly as a result of poor decision making. This innate capacity of the heart is referred to several times in The Bible. An example of this can be found in Isaiah.

> .....When the enemy shall come in like a flood, the Spirit
> of the Lord shall lift up a standard against him.
> **Isaiah 59:19**
> [KJV]

If you check the Hebrew word used here for 'flood', you'll realize that the scripture is not talking about the enemy's flood, but instead it's God's flood which sweeps away the enemy and his works.

The word used here is *'nahar'*, which translates into English as *great waters*, or God's *running waters*. It can also mean *prosperity, sparkle,* and *cheerful.*

The punctuation has been misplaced in our translation – please do your own research, but the scripture should read like this:

> .....When the enemy shall come in; like a flood [nahar] the
> Spirit of the Lord shall lift up a standard against him.
> **Isaiah 59:19**
> [KJV]

It's a small matter of grammar, but it makes a big difference to the understanding. The imagery we have is the enemy; the prince of the power of the air, coming in through our 5 senses - something we saw, or were told. Something we can't see or haven't heard in a long time, which affects our soul: our mind and emotions are affected, and our will is moreover, not far behind. At this point, The Spirit of God raises up a standard, and out from our belly (our spirit man – [Proverbs 20:27]) shall flow rivers of living water - *'nahar'*, which through the conduit of the heart, will flood the soul, and wash the enemy's influence away. Please refer to the diagram on page 5 to fully understand this powerful illustration. This is how a pure and diligently kept heart reacts to the enemy! The Nahar raises a standard, literally baptizing the soul into the comfort of knowing that God is in ultimate control.

> May the God of hope fill you with all joy and peace as you trust in him,
> so that you may overflow with hope by the power of the Holy Spirit.
> **Romans 15:13**
> [KJV]

If the heart is dysfunctional, i.e. in THC, the enemy comes in, and because the heart resonates or empathizes with the situation, instead of allowing The Word of God to flow out of it, the heart literally closes its gates to The Word of God, and inclines its ear to listen to the reasoning of the enemy, becoming even more infected, deepening the condition. The heart will eventually rupture, and the soured word of deception, will infect the spirit. Whether we want to admit it or not, this is what happens to the majority of us, on a daily basis. We need to check the condition of our hearts.

<u>THE COURT OF GOD</u>

In its office and function, the heart represents the seat or *court* of judgment. Whereas the mind may perceive a thing via its five senses, the heart will judge, or discern a thing. Schematically speaking, the heart sits right at the center of the soul, spirit and body, as an interpreter, a mediator and a modulator of truth. In our lives, we may be presented with many 'facts', but it is the heart's job to buffer this information with and against the truth. This means that our understanding should not be based upon experience in the traditional sense, but as a result of a revelation of truth. Jeremiah 17:9 tells us that the heart of man is desperately wicked – this is why we: **1)** equip our *court* with *knowledge*, by 'hiding' the law, or word of God in our heart [Psalm 19:11], and **2)** we equip our *court* with *understanding*, by inaugurating one who is able to **comprehend** the law – The Holy Spirit, who dwells in our heart as the ultimate discerner and judge. In this sense, when you operate from the (yielded) heart, you are truly operating out of the court or the *Counsel of God.*

A courtroom without a judge is like a bus without a driver: it is only a matter of time before someone unqualified takes the wheel, in an attempt to assist the bus in carrying out its function. Likewise, a Courtroom with a judge, but no law for the Judge to enforce, is like the same bus, this time with a driver, but no fuel. This aptly describes the effects of THC upon the heart of man. The reality is, buses are purpose built vehicles, and if bus drivers or fuel are suddenly taken out of the picture, the *demand* placed upon the *function* of the bus does not change. Imagine the chaos which would ensue if bus drivers just walked out of their busses in your city tomorrow, or if there was suddenly no fuel – commuters still need to get from A to B, and so it would only be a matter of time before necessity; the mother of invention, inspired the commuters into manipulating (or conditioning) the bus to carry out (a version of) its function, without the usual mandatory requirements.

It is the place where matters are reconciled and understood. Solomon says 'the fool says in his heart says there is no God – notice the use of words. Solomon did not say that the fool 'considers, or thinks, there is no God, but he is literally saying that the fool has ultimately **judged, as sound**, that there is no God; the heart being the seat of judgment. Another scriptural example of this, can be found in Luke 2:19. After the experience of the birth of Christ, whilst the shepherds and everyone who the shepherds had told was in a state of amazement; the scripture says, "but Mary kept all these things, *and pondered them in her heart.*" She wasn't reactionary, but took time for sober consideration to weigh or judge, **in her heart**, what had just occurred. Hebrews 11:11 reinforces the point that Sara *"received strength to conceive seed, and was delivered of a child when she was past age, because she **judged** Him faithful who had promised".* The ability of the heart to discern or judge is clearly a very important process, not only in our relationship with God, but also in our daily interactions with others.

So in talking about the heart as the court of God, we broach the topic of judgment. This is a word with many negative connotations, but the ability to judge is actually extremely necessary, and Biblically sound. Consider this infamous scripture:

> 'Judge not, lest ye be judged'
> Matthew 7:1

The text is not saying we should not judge – in reality, God has given us eyes, ears, a nose, taste buds and numerous sensory receptors (our 5 natural senses) which we use every day to 'judge' or discern the time of day, or which clothes to wear relative to the temperature, or even to assess or 'judge' danger. To judge matters pertaining to the spirit and ultimate truth, we have also been provided with the apparatus for the job – a heart. The correct interpretation of the scripture can be derived from the original olde English meaning.

The sentence is not structured as a warning, but rather as an instruction. The "lest ye <u>be</u>" subjunctive was a common way of phrasing 'unless you <u>are</u>'. The scriptural understanding is therefore:

[Concerning a matter], unless you are judged/ circumspect/ subject to God, do not attempt to discern, alleviate or speak with any depth concerning another, or another's situation.

This same sentiment is echoed in Jeremiah 23:18 (standing in the council of God) & John 7:24 (Jesus tells us how to Judge). For too long, Christians have allowed themselves to be muted into submission by believers and non-believers alike, who brandish this scripture as a red card, concerning matters which are clearly not reflecting the glory of God, and need God ordered judgment or discernment, in order to effect change. By doing this, we allow ourselves to become a "passive Christian" (which is in and of itself an oxymoron). There is a time an season for tongue biting, yes – however, there is a much neglected time and season in which we, as

Christians, need to take up boldness and establish our voice for the things and the ways of God. Ironically it is this same *court of God*, which will allow you to discern the difference.

The 'Court System'

Although the heart sits at the center of the soul, spirit and body as a modulator and interpreter of truth; there is a very specific flow of command – all three components do not have equal jurisdiction in the court of God. All revelation of truth originates with The Spirit of God, and is imparted to the spirit of man, whether directly (visitation, vision, spirit of prophesy, dream, Bible Study etc.), or indirectly via angels; ministering spirits or through witness, via the spirit of another person. It is the heart's job to uphold and defend the integrity of this revelation to the soul and the body, and feedback deeper levels of understanding to the spirit from what it has bought forth. Occasionally the soul and or the body will present a case before the court of God. The quality of judgment rendered back to the soul/ body, is dependent upon the quality of revelation held by the individual's spirit. Even if The Holy Spirit is seated in the court, if the revelation held by the individual's spirit is inadequate, then The (impartial) Holy Spirit, cannot rule in favor of the individual's spirit. Think of this as having a very uneducated, poorly read defense attorney, vs. an astute and articulate prosecution attorney. Even though the Judge is versed in the law, if the defense attorney has inadequately presented his case, then the Judge will have to rule in favor of the prosecution. We have seen several instances in the news in recent years, where seemingly cut and dry cases have been judged in an unexpected way, purely because of poor defense. The Court of God has only one mandate, and so above all, we MUST protect our heart. This isn't only about not opening our heart to everything and everyone, but also about respecting, honoring and upholding the 'system' of the heart. This means that we should work tirelessly to feed our spirit. Reading the word is the basis of this, but there are several other study helpers, such as sermons, books and Christian fellowship. Truly, only The Word of God, (and fellowship with The Holy Spirit), can build and properly mature ones spirit. There is NO substitute for this.

There is nothing new under the sun – truly, EVERYTHING was created in 6 days. In all we do, in all our 'creation', what we are in fact doing is just re-presenting concepts which have existed for millennia. Consider, that in the same way there are several agencies which uphold the laws kept within the high court of that land – such as the police force; in His infinite brilliance, God has provided us with several internal agencies which do exactly this for the Court of God, such as the agency of conscience. As long as the heart is kept, the issues of life flow from the heart, and the whole being; body, soul and spirit, feasts and thrives. There is no struggle in this – the heart is a purpose built 'instrument', created with its function very much at the center of its design, by the <u>greatest architect, ever.</u>

<u>NEW WINE</u>

Neither is new wine put in old wineskins; for if it is, the skins burst and are torn in pieces, and the wine is spilled and the skins are ruined. But new wine is put into fresh wineskins, and so both are preserved.
Matthew 9:17
[AMP]

Many major issues and much strife within the body of Christ arise, and stay, because we do not take heed to this scripture. We take on the teachings of Christ, we become 'saved', identifying ourselves as believers, YET what we have done, is EXACTLY what the scripture warns against. By not allowing God to renew our inner most parts, we have poured new wine, into an old wineskin. To explain the issue with this, we need to understand what the literal meaning of the scripture is.

Wineskins were traditionally used to store new wine, or as a vehicle when it was being transported. This wine could be for personal use, or for wine offerings to be taken to the temple. When the new wine was poured into the wineskin, it would mature, as it continued to ferment. In the process of fermentation, as yeast turns the sugars from the pressed grapes into alcohol, carbon dioxide gas is produced. Heat acts as a catalyst, and speeds this reaction up; so you can imagine, in a Mediterranean climate, inside an animal skin, there would be huge volumes of carbon dioxide being produced. Because of the nature of an animal membrane, gas can diffuse through the microscopic pores in the new wineskin. This is a slow process, and so when the rate of carbon dioxide production is greater than the rate of diffusion across the membrane, due to its malleability, the new wineskin is able to expand, taking on a new appearance, relative to its contents. In an old wineskin, the membrane has condensed and hardened, and therefore can neither expand to accommodate the volume of gas, nor can it carry out diffusion, and will therefore eventually burst.

	New Wineskin	Old Wineskin
Appearance	Flexible, yields to the shape of liquid poured in.	Dry and hardened into a specific, non-changeable shape, by the pervious wine. Tough, shell-like.

What happens when new wine is poured in?	The wineskin takes a new form, relative to the wine poured in. As the wine 'breathes', and becomes more mature, the new wineskin has the capacity to adapt.	The old wineskin is hardened, almost like a big plastic jug. It is still able to hold the wine, however, as the wine ferments; the gas eventually forces the old wineskin to rupture.
As a transportation device	Easy to carry, molds and adapts to the landscape of the carriers side/back, ensuring even weight distribution.	Cumbersome – hard to carry. The wine thrashes around inside the wine skin 'shell' with every movement.
Taste of wine	Sweet, mature, strong wine. The tannins* have been allowed to mature, and so impart a smoothness and depth to the wine.	Bitter, because of the tannins* left behind from the previous wine. It's also unlikely that the wine was able to mature fully, due to the old wineskin splitting. Without discernment, this will look like matured, full-bodied wine, because of the dark color imparted by the tannins*.

* - What are tannins?

When it comes to winemaking, tannins are a family of organic compounds found in the seeds, skin and stem of a grape. They are natural antioxidants and preservatives, and once properly matured, impart a richness and depth to the wine. Their characteristic taste is astringent, bitter, or dry, causing the mouth and back of the throat to pucker. This taste is referred to as 'tannic'. Tannins will initially impart this 'tannic' quality to a wine, but over time, as the wine goes through a process of maturation, the tannins will impart smoothness and depth, making it more palatable. The profile of tannins in a wine are specific to that harvest of grapes, however, if you were to mix the tannins from a previous batch of grapes, with the current harvest, the result would be an unpleasantly bitter, acrid wine. This is another issue with the old wineskin – contamination.

We need to realize, that it is not enough to simply go to church, read our Bible, read Christian literature, listen to Christian music, pray, fast.... There is a point at which we need to put our faith into action; and believing all the fantastic stuff which The Bible says about us, who we are, and the relationship God desires with us; prepare ourselves a worthy vessel of said word – remember, The Bible says faith without works, is dead. The reality is that God's word CAN be poured into an old wineskin, or a heart which resonates more with the past that it came from, than the reality of Jesus Christ: being loved, being saved and set free. However, this will always result in the word eventually bursting out, tainted, bitter, and not edifying to the place to which it would have been carried, nor to the vessel which carried it. The unchanged heart CANNOT hold/contain the word of God. Another way of expressing that, is; Gods word cannot be applied to a life, which has been hardened in the things the past has taught it. If our foundation is wrong, then no matter how fantastic the edifice built on top, it will eventually crumble. Herein we have the difference between *basic comprehension*, and *the lifestyle of Christ*. This is very evident in the body today, where we have the greatest revelation of love, ever expressed; yet we are unable to facilitate this same love to our families and congregants, let alone the world. Like a malnourished mother whose breasts can no longer produce milk for her baby; you cannot express what is not IN you. Selah.

Many times, these old wineskins are perceived as wisdom – they are after all, tried and tested, and have been faithful in the past. They contain the antioxidant/ preservative tannins, and so we hold onto the old wineskins, believing that they will enhance the new wine; missing the revelation that it is the new wine, incomparable to any other substance we have handled before, which will enhance the wineskin, and not the other way around – the wine preserves it! A wineskin only becomes an old wineskin, once the wine is removed, and it desiccates. There are several therapeutic substances in wine, including *resveratrol*; a compound which has been at the center of longevity studies for over 2 decades. Amongst its list of purported effects are improved heart health, and the ability to preserve the integrity of tissue, whilst protecting it from undesirable external factors. There are many behaviors and habits that we pick up – protective measures with the aim of preventing traumas such as loneliness, hurt and being treated like a doormat, but even though these are hailed as wisdom by the wider world, they are not of God. His 'new wine' is sufficient, and contains everything you require; meeting, and even surpassing to meet your needs. It is time to let go, and to let God in.

I recently heard a very well known pastor, speak on international Christian television, saying that she would not share her money with her husband if she married – she worked hard for what she has, and therefore they will have to have separate bank accounts. She then went on to say she would not be cooking or cleaning for him, and he would need to get a maid if he required any of those services. Now, the intricacies and agreements of every relationship are different – two consenting adults will justifiably 'find their level', which will ultimately determine how they interact as a couple. But the fact that this pastor, before even entering into a relationship, was so blinkeredly adamant in her stance, represents a perfect case study of an individual who is manifesting the fruit of an old wineskin. Those old tannins, manifesting in the new wine; tainted and unfit for consumption, or an offering. As she spoke from her old wineskin; outside of *The Counsel of God*, and the audience applauded her 'realness', my mind was bought to the words of 2 Timothy 3:6-7:

> ⁶For of this sort are they which creep into houses, and lead captive silly women laden with sins, led away with divers lusts, ⁷Ever learning, and never able to come to the knowledge of the truth.
> **2 Timothy 3:6-7**
> [KJV]

And to clarify, the impetus upon using this scripture wasn't based upon the fact that this was indeed an audience of women – this has <u>nothing</u> to do with gender. WE collectively are the bride of Christ, and whether male female [Galatians 3:28], we all have the capacity to become 'silly women, led away with divers lusts', and sadly there are those, in leadership, who will lead *silly women* captive, through the vehicle of emotionalism - preaching from (and to) the old wineskin – after all, deep calls to deep and iron sharpens iron. THC is a *systemic* problem, and so even as write this, I'm reminded about how inter-connected this all is. The systems of THC are really, all the same, but the manifestations are all just slightly different. The problem of the old wineskin, also speaks of empathy, which is discussed more thoroughly, in **chapter 6**.

It's ironic, because old wineskin looks like scar tissue – dried, inflexible, darkened, thickened skin. Scar tissue replaces regular tissue, and is a part of the body's healing response to trauma. Because of its rigidity, it tears easily, which is exactly what happens when an old wineskin ruptures. When I researched scar tissue, one of the things that stood out to me, is the fact that it is significantly less receptive to the UV radiation from sunlight than healthy tissue, and that light itself becomes an irritant to scar tissue - this is the problem with the old wineskin! The Bible says:

> And the light shineth in darkness; and the darkness comprehended it not.
> **John 1:5**
> [KJV]

This is because the scar tissue resonates more with the trauma, than it does with its function – as tissue; in the same way that an old wineskin, or a wounded heart empathizes more with its past, and so cannot comprehend, contain or process the new wine: God's light of truth. Healthy tissue has the capacity to interact with, and be receptive to the entire electromagnetic spectrum of light, adapting itself accordingly; however scar tissue doesn't remember its original function, and so 'strange behavior' is observed when it is exposed to light. This 'strange behavior' can manifest in a multitude of ways; stubbornness to Godly rebuke, pride and ego being some of the most virulent.

I pray that The Holy Sprit would expose and remove every old wineskin in your life, that you would experience God's rich depth of sweetness, and go on to impart no bitter in all that you do.

RECEIPTS (MANASSEH)

> And Joseph called the name of the firstborn Manasseh: For God, said he, hath made me forget all my toil, and all my father's house.
> **Genesis 41:51**
> [KJV]

This section is about forgiveness, and how the seed of unforgiveness, can intrinsically poison the quality of ones life. In THC, we tend to be incapable of letting go of the past. New revelation comes, and we embrace it, in part, but we insist on taking the past with us - receipts. The human revelation is vast, and much like the old wineskin in the previous section, has proved itself to be true in the past – to cast down the old flesh isn't an easy feat, and the reality is people don't often really want to. In our limited perception, the revelation of the flesh keeps us from getting hurt. We need to understand a truth:

> ***The revelation of the flesh, is the <u>antithesis</u> to the revelation of Christ.***

For example – the individual, who has been abused by men in power, physically, mentally or even sexually, has their own set of receipts. This person understands that men in power can be malevolent, and as such, with their revelation, will be careful to avoid any interactions with them. The revelation of Christ takes us from a place of knowledge and experience, to a place of wisdom beyond experience. It is very apparent to see how difficult it would be to transpose from these 'receipts' - the 'wisdom' of the revelation of the flesh, to the wisdom of the revelation of Christ, which instructs us to emphatically forget the past, and now move forward in the knowledge of the love of Christ ONLY. [Isaiah 43:18-19, 2 Corinthians 5:17, Ephesians 4:31-32, Philippians 3:13 & 4:6].

Someone in the Bible who could be perceived as justified in 'keeping receipts' was Joseph. He had every reason to be bitter, guarded, untrusting – he endured a lot. Growing up in a family of men, the tenth son – the first brother born by Rachael, 'dad's other wife'; the likelihood is that he dealt with rejection from an early age. Joseph came from what we would probably call a dysfunctional home today. At the age of six, he witnessed his brothers pillage and murder the men of an entire Canaanite city, including King Hamor and his son Shechem, after it transpired that his older sister Dinah had fornicated with her lover, Shechem: think Romeo and Juliet, star crossed, forbidden-inter-tribal love. Joseph's brothers were thugs. There would have been a great struggle for identity, only compounded by the fact that at the tender age of 7 years old, Joseph's mother Rachael died, causing Jacob to isolate Joseph and his baby brother Benjamin as 'favorites'. Joseph started to have dreams – dreams that he possibly thought would make him more of a star to his brothers, but simply made the tension worse. Shortly after, his own brothers stripped him of his multicolored jacket - an expensive gift from his father, put him into a pit, and sold him into slavery. He arrived in Egypt and became Potiphar's slave. After years of hard work, Joseph was promoted, only to catch the roaming eye of Potiphar's wife, who tried to seduce him. Joseph did the right thing, but was thrown in prison after Potiphar's wife lied and said he attacked her. [Please bear in mind that in line with the cultural tradition of the day, it would have been customary for Joseph to be made a eunuch before he was allowed into Potiphar's compound (so that he could be trusted with female family members). IF Joseph wasn't castrated prior to entering Potiphar's house, then in line with tradition, he definitely should have been as punishment for the alleged attack. In the Hebrew text, the word *'saris'* is used to describe him – a word generally meaning slave, but more commonly used to denote an individual castrated for service - a eunuch. It is baffling therefore that Joseph goes on to have children. In this light, it is extremely likely that, short of a miracle; Joseph's children were adopted or conceived by a paternal surrogate. IF indeed Joseph was castrated as a result of his brothers selling him into slavery, this was yet another reason for him to keep receipts]. Joseph was incarcerated for many years, and whilst he was there he interpreted the dreams of his fellow inmates. Joseph saw many criminals incarcerated, and freed, whilst he wasted away in prison for a crime he didn't commit. Time passed, and one day, after Pharaoh's chief cupbearer made mention of Joseph, he was summoned to the palace to interpret Pharaoh's dreams. Although from this moment onwards life got better for Joseph, he had every reason to be bitter, yet not only was he able to forgive his brothers, but when he had his first son, he named him Manasseh – derived from the Hebrew root verb, *'nasha'*, meaning 'caused [me] to forget'. *Nasha* can also mean 'to lend', or 'to be a creditor' - therefore there is also a sense of the wiping of a debt that was owed to Joseph, perhaps by his brothers. Joseph left the past behind, and so was able to embrace the sweetness of what God had delivered him into.

This issue of debt is a major reason why many of us cannot forgive. There is a wicked element of the human psyche, which perceives that it is a good thing to have people indebted to you. I'd call it a *God complex*, where rather than wanting to 'walk in a God-like place' as it pertains to Holiness and Righteousness, we want to 'walk in a God-like place', as it pertains to being owed a great debt. We shun His nature, but desire His *fame* – the same mistake Lucifer made. Many people battle this, and are so poisoned by unforgiveness that they seem to gain pleasure from holding onto the past, whilst it usurps and sucks true sweetness away from every aspect of their life. At this juncture, with reference to Deuteronomy 15:6 and 28:12-13 – 'a lender and not a borrower', I'd like point out that the blessing spoken of in these verses, is a counteraction to the curse of being one who needs to borrow. The blessing is therefore nothing to do with being a lender, but first and foremost to be in a position of liberty from the human tendency toward indebtedness (the curse), and therefore actually have enough that you can become a blessing; a (glad) lender. The blessing is manifested into our lives as an understanding of abundance wherein debt (even that of an apology) is not our portion, but out of the abundance of our heart (because it is not us who live, but Christ who lives in and through us), we are still able to extend more – *even* when this *seems* nonsensical. This is *exactly* the quality Jesus was talking about in Luke 6:29 and Matthew 5:39 – offering the other cheek.

The reality is, the one who threw the arrow is seldom the one to remove it and tend to the wound(s) created. The paradigm of debt as it pertains to forgiveness, locks us into a false system of perceived entitlement, which negates and blinds us to our genuine entitlement, through Christ, as sons and daughters in The Kingdom - to walk in complete *sozo* (see Chapter 2 – Salvation). Deliverance - even from a tragic past; healing – even from the words and actions of loved ones, which pierced so deep that some 20 years later, the scars still remain; and salvation – securely resolute in the perfect shalom of God.

Just as we have been forgiven, Jesus calls us to forgive. Never let the following scriptures depart from the inward meditation of your heart.

> [21] Then came Peter to him, and said, Lord, how oft shall my brother sin against me, and I forgive him? till seven times?

²² Jesus saith unto him, I say not unto thee, Until
seven times: but, Until seventy times seven.
Matthew 18:21-22
[KJV]

²³ So if when you are offering your gift at the altar you there
remember that your brother has any [grievance] against you,
²⁴ Leave your gift at the altar and go. First make peace with
your brother, and then come back and present your gift.
Matthew 5:23-24
[AMP]

And be not conformed to this world: but be ye transformed
by the renewing of your mind, that ye may prove what [is]
that good, and acceptable, and perfect, will of God.
Romans 12:2
[KJV]

CHAPTER 2

COMPARTMENTALIZATION

A false balance is abomination to the Lord: but a just weight is his delight.
Proverbs 11:1

"Compartmentalization is an unconscious psychological defense mechanism used to avoid *cognitive dissonance*, or the mental discomfort and anxiety caused by a person's having conflicting values, cognitions, emotions, beliefs, etc. within themselves. Compartmentalization allows these conflicting ideas to co-exist by inhibiting direct or explicit acknowledgement and interaction

-T. Leary, M. Leary and Price -
Handbook of self and identity [June ed.].

More simply put, compartmentalization is a phenomena in which an individual (often unconsciously) breaks down aspects of their reality, which may be disharmonious or difficult to conceive or contend with, into easier to deal with 'compartments'. It often manifests as a psychosis, born out of an individual's inability, *or refusal* to digest **whole, balanced truth**. Essentially, this is what a computer does, when it compresses, or 'zips' data due to its large volume. This data is for the most part, disjointed gibberish in its zipped state, and it is not until the dots are connected, and this information is extrapolated, or 'rehydrated', that we get the true, originally intended understanding. Compartmentalization allows individuals to cope with the reality of a seemingly complex situation, and can be completely normal and healthy as a 'transitory' state, but becomes an issue when an individual doesn't, **a)** build the picture back up, and/or **b)** has compartmentalized or 'fractionated' sight, and so compartmentalizes *everything* as their natural state of being. Because of the way we have been educated, and the effect of media; creating an increasingly narcissistic society, globally, we are losing grasp of the whole picture. Both examples, **a)** and **b)**, are unfortunately now commonplace.

God always deals with the whole picture: the family, the church, the nation – even when it comes down to the individual; God is concerned with the whole individual, as opposed to just one aspect. In our churches and our homes, leadership is imparted from God, to *the head* downward, but glory is given back up to God, from the *feet up* [Prov. 17:6]. The problem with compartmentalization is that when leadership is imparted from God to *the head*, downward, by the time it reaches to *the feet*, it has become fragmented, and so no longer makes any sense. *The feet* do not understand the compartmentalized interpretation of what was intended by God, for *the head* to transmit to them, and so a 'strange' glory, is therefore all that is left remaining to offer back up to God. This is, in a very literal sense, <u>a false balance</u>.

For an actual example of this compartmentalized comprehension, we may as well start at the beginning: in Genesis with the creation of Adam and Eve. In the beginning God **created** Adam. Genesis 5:2 tells us that:

> **Male** *and* **female** *created He* **them**; *and blessed* **them**, <u>*and*</u> <u>*called* **their** *name* **Adam**</u>, *in the* **day** *when* **they** *were created.*

<u>Eve was not a second creation.</u> Please re-read the text. The original Adam was split into two 'Adams', one retaining the name Adam, one being named Eve, or *'Chava'* in Hebrew, connected with the word *'Chai'* meaning life and *'Chaya'*, meaning living. She

was separated from, or *from out of* Adam to be a help meet to him [Gen 2:20] – The Bible says God took a rib from Adam and *made* a woman for Adam. [Gen. 2:21-22]. The word *made* denotes the act of taking a pre-existing thing, or things to a different interpretation, as opposed to create, which speaks of elucidating or establishing something out of vast nothingness. The original Adam, created (and *made*, from clay) on the 6th day, comprised both male and female; ask **any** Jew - this was always the understanding. The story is often depicted in Jewish art, representing Adam as a 'Siamese twin' (a non-literal representation of a being who would later be split into two), but in Christendom we have compartmentalized the understanding to mean that Eve was created at a later date. Eve was there (as part of the original Adam), when God commanded Adam not to eat from *The Tree of the Knowledge of Good and Evil*, and so was fully aware when she allowed herself to be seduced into partaking. This, to illustrate the fact that we need to go back to the start, and truly ask The Holy Spirit to rebuild every incomplete and compartmentalized understanding; line upon line, precept upon precept; that we would know Him and manifest a more perfect love toward Him, in understanding.

SALVATION

Salvation, through Christ, is what makes us Christians. It is the most pivotal thing that will ever happen in an individual's life; in fact, <u>salvation is life,</u> *and* a lifestyle. Unfortunately, because of the way we were educated, and because of the structure of the English language, many of us 'fall at the first hurdle' when it comes to fully understanding the true meaning of what it is to be saved. Salvation, saved, savior are words we use all the time, but for the most part, we have a compartmentalized comprehension of what it is to be saved, and because this is a matter of language and education, we propagate the misunderstanding weekly in our church services, in our Bible studies, and generationally, to our children in our homes and in Sunday Schools around the world. It means that we have an incomplete understanding of what it is to be saved, and more importantly, it affects our heart and deforms our reality into something God had not intended. When you were saved, what was the promise? What does the word mean?

The word used in The Bible denoting salvation, is the Greek word *sozo*. Directly translated into English, *sozo* actually means not just salvation from hell; but Salvation, AND Healing, AND Deliverance. Please understand that when God saves *(sozos)* you, the reality is that you were healed, saved, and delivered at the same time: delivered from demonic oppression, poverty, healed from sickness, anger, depression, and saved from the wages of sin, which is death. This may sound a million miles away from what you have always been taught, but it is a truth evident throughout scripture.

Salvation	Healing	Deliverance
For the Son of man is come to seek and to save [**sozo**] that which was lost. Luke 19:10 KJV	For she said within herself, If I may but touch his garment, I shall be whole [**sozo**]. Matthew 9:21 KJV	I will therefore put you in remembrance, though ye once knew this, how that the Lord, having delivered [**sozo**] the people out of the land of Egypt, afterward destroyed them that believed not. **Jude 1:5 KJV**

For God sent not his Son into the world to condemn the world; but that the world through him might be saved [*sozo*]. John 3:17 KJV	And he said unto him, Arise, go thy way: thy faith hath made thee whole [*sozo*]. Luke 17:19 KJV	And the Lord will deliver [*sozo*] me from every evil work and preserve me for His heavenly kingdom. To Him be glory forever and ever. Amen! 2 Timothy 4:18 KJV
That if thou shalt confess with thy mouth the Lord Jesus, and shalt believe in thine heart that God hath raised him from the dead, thou shalt be saved [*sozo*]. Romans 10:9 KJV	Then Jesus said to him, "Receive your sight; your faith has made you well [*sozo*]." Luke 18:42 KJV	And they that saw it told them how he that was possessed with demons was made whole [*sozo*]. Luke 8:36 KJV

There are 111 other examples in The Bible (120 in total) that you can research in your own personal study.

Jesus did not only pay for your salvation [sozo]; Jesus IS salvation [sozo – healing, deliverance, and salvation]. To experience sozo, is to experience Jesus.

When we compartmentalize salvation, we lose out – many Christians, by the definition of *sozo*, are unfortunately only one third saved. Everything God does is holistic. Salvation [*sozo*] is holistic, that we might experience salvation in our spirit, deliverance in our soul and healing in our body. Remember, these are all the same thing, and so please don't focus on the semantics of whether one's soul is in fact delivered, or saved or if it is the spirit or the body which is healed - it is all *SOZO*. Whilst we may have seen, or experienced something different in our personal lives and in ministry, we cannot re-interpret The Word of God, based upon experience. The truth is unchallengeable, and cannot be changed.

The Bible says two cannot walk together if they are unequally yoked. An individual who is saved in the spirit, yet not healed in the body, or delivered in the mind/ soul is a recipe for a lifetime of

struggle. Two aspects (minimum) have to be under *sozo* (although all three aspects is obviously the ideal). Truly, the individual who is saved in the spirit, yet not in the soul, will eventually run into ruin. The same could be said about someone not experiencing *sozo* in their body/ in the physical realm - The Bible believing saved (in the spirit, because she

confesses Jesus as Lord) woman, who in the unrelenting pain of her terminal condition, requests assisted suicide, and has therefore let her physical situation seduce her soul into usurping her spirit, to a point where she no longer wants to live. A less extreme, possibly more relatable example; we all need food, raiment, and shelter, which The Bible says come from God. The person who hasn't experienced the reality of this aspect of *sozo* in their physical life, will spend more time working in a typical week, than they will in the meditative worship of God. Their soul (the mind, the will, *the emotions*) becomes dominant, and the spirit is demoted, as the individual's 'worship' of work/ their need for money, surpasses their worship of, and need for God. This in turn affects faith, which wears down belief to a point when an individual no longer has the time, energy or inclination to confess the words and sentiment of Psalm 20:7, "Some trust in chariots, and some in horses: but we will remember the name of the Lord our God".

The spirit, the soul, the body: if two of these are not equally yoked in *sozo*, there is a big issue. The aspect(s) of yourself which is/ are not in *sozo*, will continually undermine the aspect(s) of yourself which is/are in *sozo*, and vice versa. Two cannot walk together unless they are equally yoked, and whilst we are alive all three aspects (that's three sets of two – the soul and the spirit, the spirit and the body, the body and the soul) <u>must</u> live together, and so there will be a constant pull; the soul trying to put its yoke on the body; the body trying to put its yoke on the spirit and so on... If **two** aspects are in *sozo*, it is likely that the **third** aspect will also be yoked into *sozo*, but if **two** aspects are <u>NOT in *sozo*</u>, it is likely, that in time, the **third** aspect will be subdued and taken OUT of *sozo*.

Paul lets us know in 1 Corinthians 15:50-55, that the mortal body cannot inherit The Kingdom of God, and that on the Day of Judgment, we will be CHANGED, from a mortal [body], to an immortal [body]. The Greek word for changed here, is *allagēsometha*, which is to change the execution of a thing, to update, or to create a variance of an existing thing. The word is also used in Acts 6:14; *"For we have heard him say, that this Jesus of Nazareth shall destroy this place, and shall **change** [allagēsometha] the customs which Moses delivered us"*. Please note, that just as the scripture above differentiates between destroy and change [*allagēsometha*], in Corinthians 15:51, the body is not being destroyed, but changed/ updated – <u>we will still have a body</u>. It is also fitting to acknowledge that Jesus did indeed change the laws of Moses, or as Matthew 5:15 puts it, *Think not that I am come to destroy the law, or the prophets: I am not come to destroy, but to fulfil.* Jesus did not do away with the laws, but Calvary bought them into new light and a higher interpretation. Salvation itself works BECAUSE of the law, not independently of it. The laws were a shadow of things to come (Hebrews 10:1), just like our mortal bodies. We are a single manifestation of life, with three 'understandings', like Our Father, I AM, the author of our creation. We are not being downsized, but changed into a different single manifestation of those three understandings.

31

A similar sentiment can be seen in the scripture below:

And the very God of peace sanctify you wholly; and I pray
*God your **whole** spirit **and** soul **and body** be preserved*
blameless unto the coming of our Lord Jesus Christ.
1 Thessalonians 5:23 (KJV)

This brings us to an interesting realization. The Bible says:

"On the evidence of two witnesses or of three witnesses the one who is
to die shall be put to death; a person shall not be put to death on the
evidence of one witness."
-Deuteronomy 17:6 (KJV)

The fact is; all three *witnesses* will be present on the Day of Judgment. The Spirit, the Soul, and the Body. For one, an individual will not be put to death, but for two or three.

"My friend Karen is such a good person! She doesn't believe in
Jesus, but her heart is golden. She is a real, genuine person.
Karen volunteers in her community, she loves her family,
and she doesn't believe in fornication – she said she is waiting
for marriage! She puts some Christians to shame"...

Besides the fact that it is not given to man, to judge who is "good", and that good works do not equate to salvation; this is an example of someone who exhibits the *image/* appearance of *sozo* in her soul (only God can judge if what she appears to be exhibiting is actually *sozo*), However, without confessing Jesus, her spirit witnesses against her.

We always think of judgment with negative connotations, but judgment is simply another way of expressing a test. When The Bible tells us to test every spirit, we are being told to judge the intentions of that spirit, relative to the word of God. When you sit a test, you are being judged relative to what you (should have) studied: what's in you? Judging/ testing is always against a standard. A few weeks after a seed is put into the earth (generally speaking), the judgment/ test verifies the seed, by the fact that a shoot has sprung up out of the place where it was originally planted - the same is true for what happens nine months after a man and woman consummate their relationship. Judgment is a neutral process. Negative outcomes are not because you were judged - they are because of what happened before judgment, and vice versa positive outcomes. On the Day of Judgment, Christ is the standard. Am I in you? First witness, take the stand...

> "For where **two** or **three** are gathered *in my name*,
> there am I among them."
> Matt. 18:20

When Jesus spoke to the woman whose daughter was vexed with a demon in Matthew 15:21-28, He made a statement that, 'It is not meet to take the children's bread, and to cast it to dogs.' We understand that at this time, Jesus was ministering to the House of Israel exclusively, however, understanding this statement from an eschatological slant; Jesus was saying that within *sozo*, those who are spirit-saved (the children), are nourished and sustained by healing and deliverance - it is their daily bread; their food – this is an illustrative definition of *sozo*, or balanced/ whole salvation. This food is prepared and laid up in abundance beyond measure, and so the issue is not quantity. Every time a non-spirit-saved person is delivered, or healed; they feast on the bread of the children, a food which does not line up with their destiny. It is only by grace that a non-believer is healed whilst refusing salvation, and every time this happens it creates a false balance: an abomination. Someone living an abhorrent life, who doesn't confess Christ, yet receives healing [*sozo*], has 'tasted' salvation [sozo], yet declined its call, and therefore heaped coals upon their own head. Partial salvation is not any of ours goal, and I pray that even as salvation *[sozo]* has been extended toward all mankind, that this day, you would choose to luxuriate in the fullness of all that Calvary gave you access to.

> *I call heaven and earth to record this day against you,*
> *that I have set before you life and death, blessing*
> *and cursing: therefore choose life, that both thou*
> *and thy seed may live. – Deuteronomy 30:19*

(THE) FRUIT OF THE SPIRIT

> [22] But the **fruit** of the Spirit **is** love, joy, peace,
> longsuffering, gentleness, goodness, faith,
> [23] Meekness, temperance: against such there is no law.
> **Galatians 5:22-23**
> [KJV]

How many fruit are being described here? Please re-read the scripture, noting the emphasis on *fruit* and *is* (as opposed to *fruits* and *are*). The answer is one – **one fruit**. The Greek word used here for "fruit" is "*karpos*" and it is in the singular - Galatians 5:22-23 describes the (nine) attributes of a SINGLE fruit: love, joy, peace, longsuffering, gentleness, goodness, faith, meekness and temperance. In the same way that one could talk about an orange (a single fruit) and describe the attributes or components as being rind, pith, flesh, stem, fragrance, taste, color, texture and seeds – that's nine attributes, but one fruit. If I have the rind and the seeds of an orange, I do not have an orange; similarly if I have all the components, but they are not correctly integrated, i.e.: a pile of flesh, some seeds, pith, a stem, citrus fragrance, citrus taste, orange color, 'juicy' texture, and some rind, I still do not have the complete fruit. Simply put, if you don't display all nine attributes in a whole, integrated form; you are not manifesting The Fruit of The Spirit! Throughout The Bible, the righteous are likened to trees, obvious examples being Psalm 1:3 and Proverbs 11:30. In Galatians 5:22, Paul describes to us the exact fruit (singular) a tree of righteousness (a true child of God) bears. This has always been interesting to me, because most of the literature, and most of the presentations for the topic of The Fruit of The Spirit, will somewhere contain an image of a tree, with nine different fruit on it. Trees do not (naturally) bear different types of fruit, but bear a single *type* of fruit, after its kind. For many, this is a hard fruit to swallow (pun intended), and it is an easier path to choose one/ a handful of the nine attributes instead, and call these fruit. However, do not be deceived – God is not the author of confusion.

I have sat in so many Bible study classes and sermons on The Fruit of The Spirit, and it was always presented to me as the FRUIT(S) of the spirit. I had even been taught that no one has all of the 'fruits', and even participated in a quiz to determine 'which fruits' I possessed. At some point, it seems we have broken the fruit up into mini fruit, meaning an individual could be justified, operating in gentleness for example, but without love and with no goodness - think of the stories we hear about the sadistic nuns in Catholic boarding schools, cold and mean hearted; lacking love, yet gentle and meek. This is not the will of God. When the fruit manifests, all aspects of the fruit are simultaneously present. In a Christocentric understanding, it is a contradiction to say that one can operate in an aspect of the fruit, independently of the others – a false balance is an *abomination* before God. Christ manifested the fruit, in all he did, and in doing so, set the only standard as it pertains to The Fruit of The Spirit. An example of this 'whole fruit' relationship can be found in 1 Corinthians 13:4-7, which speaks of love as being: patient (longsuffering/ self control), kind (goodness) does not dishonor others (gentleness) it does not boast/ is not proud/ is not self-seeking (meekness) does not delight in evil (temperance) but rejoices in truth (joy) always trusts, always hopes (faith) always protects and always preserves (peace). Love, and the whole fruit of the spirit are indelibly, inseparably synonymous – you cannot truly express love if you are not one who manifests The Fruit of The Spirit.

Another reason for the misconceptions about The Fruit of The Spirit, is that people tend to get The *Fruit* and The *Gifts* of The Spirit mixed up. The Fruit of The Spirit is one, but The Gifts of The Spirit are many, including speaking in tongues, interpretation of tongues, prophecy and the discerning of spirits. The Fruit of The Spirit, expressed in and through an individual's life, is evidence that the Holy Spirit dwells in that individual. By their <u>fruit</u>, you will know them.

It is my intense prayerful desire that you would experience in your life and lifestyle, the full and constant manifestation of THE FRUIT of The Spirit.

THE GREAT I AM

God is the same yesterday, today, tomorrow, and forever – we know this to be true from scripture. However, if we are honest, that statement appears to be contradictory, relative to what is written of the '*Old Testament God'* who would wipe out entire nations because of sin, vs. the '*God of our experience'* maybe, who when we consider the wickedness on the planet right now is *seemingly* an entirely different God.

As was stated at the beginning of this chapter, compartmentalization isn't always a bad thing – as long as the picture is reconstituted in the end. Sometimes we need to compartmentalize in order to establish and appreciate the depth of a thing. Jesus compartmentalized precepts all the time when He told parables, so that a more effective picture could be drawn to our understanding. You may also realize that dreams and visions are often given in a 'compartmentalized' form, and it is only with the Holy Spirit that we begin to discern, unpick and correctly interpret the signs, symbols and phrasings therein. This is important, because at such a time at this, I believe by the Holy Spirit that we are required to reconstitute the compartmentalized understanding of God, that we may know Him, in truth.

We speak about the Father, The Son, and The Holy Spirit/ Ghost; *"the trinity"* however this is a very juvenile, and compartmentalized understanding of God. Yes, there are three understandings of God, three reference points which help us to identify His nature, but the three are one [1 John, 5:7], and so in maturity we must have a unified understanding of one God.

> Hear, O Israel: The LORD our God is **one** LORD
> – Deut. 6:4

In order to inform our understanding, throughout time, God revealed His aspects, one at a time, so that we could understand the pieces, and then reconstitute the understandings to make a whole, balanced understanding of who God is:

El – The God of Abraham, Isaac and Jacob

The earliest (post Adamic) awareness of God was an understanding of The Holy Spirit; the divine, intangible nature of God. Remember, He is the same forever, and so it is not that He was different back then, rather that this is the aspect of His nature which was ministering to humanity, at that point in time. There are instances where, for example, Jesus shows up prior to the official dispensation of Jesus (eg: the manna of Exodus, or Shadrach, Meeshach and Abednego in the fiery furnace ~500BC), but this just further proves the point, that:

- The fullness of God already existed.
- The fullness of God had not yet been revealed.
- An element/ aspect of God, was already ministering to people on earth at this time.

In Exodus 6:2-3 God speaks to Moses, and says that Abraham, Isaac and Jacob knew Him, but under a different revelation to that which Moses understood Him. People knew, and called upon God *before* the Ten Commandments were given – they just knew a different manifestation of God. It was under Enosh, the son of Seth, that Genesis 4:6 says "then began men to call upon the name of the LORD". This was when the people called upon a God, who they knew not, had no text, no understanding; just an oral account of an experience from their great grandparents - this is when, for the first time after the fall, the Holy Spirit was called upon; the impersonal, divine essence of God.

To draw an analogy, this is when humanity was a baby, and like all babies, their first impression of their parents is a divine, intangible being, who can make food magically appear, and disappear. The baby doesn't really understand what a parent is, or their role as a baby. The baby only understands that this 'being' favors them, and will answer to their call.

*For the scholars amongst you, I'll append by saying that El is NOT the Canaanite god by the same name, but the God of the Hebrews, as referred to in scripture (El-Shaddi, **El-El**yon, Isra**El** Beth**El**, Elohim, Gabri**El**, Micha**El**), and likely comes from the Aramaic, Elah, meaning God. (It is speculated by many that El worked its way into the Hebrew vernacular after the time Israel spent in Canaan, or indeed that the worship system of Israel was taken from the Canaanites.) With a little research, this statement can be disproven.*

<u>YHVH – The God of Moses</u>

In this manifestation of God the Father – the authoritarian and provider, comes rules, laws and discipline, protection, provision and structure. In the same way that an earthly father establishes the rules of a household with his children, Father God gave rules to a juvenile nation, through Moses. This is The Father that will tell you to <u>be back by 8pm</u>, and if you deviate from that time, even slightly, there will be repercussions! This is also the father who would protect and provide for His children, doing everything to ensure that His children had the best. Under this dispensation, we see the highest instances of rules, and resultant chastisement for the breaking of rules. This is the aspect of God we respect and revere, not only because He is divine, but because He is Our Father.

This is the 'teenage' understanding of a parent, when all we seem to see is a long list of rules, and we come to the understanding that in order to have a good relationship with our parent, we need to master the art of submission – difficult, but to those who do, the rewards are great. It is silly to think that a 50-year old will still obligate themselves to an 8pm curfew, however, there are lessons which were learned in passing through the teenage dispensation when curfews were imposed; lessons which teach principles which only serve to promote or deepen our understanding of what it is to honor, to respect and to be accountable.

Jesus – The Son of God/ Son of man

Jesus came as a reminder, that as much as God is holy and set apart; as much as God is a Father, He also relates to us as a son, a brother, a friend. Jesus is the older brother, that holds the hand of his crying younger sibling, taking said sibling to see their parents for comfort and re-affirmation; the older brother who takes the blame and subsequent punishment for the dish that YOU broke. Jesus is the final understanding of God – and from a logistical standpoint, He had to be broken down to our comprehension in this order. We had to be introduced to the Holy Spirit; the absolute impersonal divinity of God FIRST, and only then could we attribute this ultimately holy God, as being The Father. It is at this point that we can understand the third nature: Jesus - the word, *in context*. It is easier to attribute personality to the divine, than it is to attribute divine – true divinity, to a personality. Familiarity breeds contempt, and so the divine has to be ordered FIRST, before we can fully appreciate sonship, which needs to be established so that we can participate in friendship with God; divine, father, friend.

This is the young adult who has moved out, and finds a new dimension to their relationship with their parents. The understanding shifts the young adult from a paradigm of 'what can my parents do for me' to, in responsibility, 'what can I do for my parents?' It is in this dispensation that an individual will be invited to understand and appreciate their parents as 'friends', as opposed to an authority figure (though authority is never forsaken).

Present day – The Fullness of God

This is the fullness of God which is talked about in Ephesians 3:19. In this present dispensation, because of Jesus, we are free to know the fullness of God, and not just an aspect.

This reminds me of The Fruit of The Spirit, in that all aspects have to be present at all times, otherwise there is a strange manifestation when the pieces are not correctly balanced.

When God the Father punished Israel, and Moses took Him to task, The Bible says that He repented of the Evil that he considered to do [Exodus 32:14] - except that Numbers 23:19 says that God is not a man, that he should lie; neither the son of man, that he should repent. This *appears* to be a contradiction. There are several examples throughout the Old Testament when God is said to *repent* [2 Samuel 24:16; 1 Chronicles 21:15; Jeremiah 18:8; Jeremiah 26:3, 13, 19; Jeremiah 42:10; Amos 7:3, 6; Jonah 3:10]. I would hypothesize that because *God The Father* was made manifest to this generation of people, but the dispensation of Jesus had not yet come, and the Holy Spirit was an 'old understanding', that this was akin to someone manifesting compassion, without love – only part of the manifestation of God, i.e. only part of the manifestation of The Fruit of the Spirit. A father loves you, but a father is not your friend - this is not his primary job. Although a father knows that you can take the punishment he just doled out, in love, sometimes he can regret the punishment, especially when the mother, his other half/ aspect gets involved. Regret, not for lack of foresight or because he went too far, but because it hurts <u>every</u> father to see his child(ren) distressed – even through the act of warranted rebuke.

When we look at the classical Pentecostal revivals, we see Jesus, the manifestation of the Holy Spirit, but we also see a resurgence of legalism (The Father) - a sign that the fullness of God had been exposed to people at that time, marking the beginning of the manifestation of The Fullness of God - the dispensation we are currently in.

Although the fullness of God was available to all to experience and know from this point onwards, understand that this was new, and so people initially created (and continue to create) strange understandings, doctrines and religious movements, in the act of trying to grapple this *new* concept of God. This is something you see all the time with children, who draw 'pictures', multi-colored interpretations of things they have by all means experienced, but their representation is very poor, such as the green, red and blue squiggle-blob interpretation of mum, and the purple-brown-green triangular interpretation of dad. Older children might paint a picture of their parents next to the family home and car; where the car is as big as a two-story house, and their stickmen parents' heads reach the roof of said house. The child has had access to the car, their parents, and their home, but does not yet understand scale and ratio, and so has issues with representing this image accurately. With time, as the child understands the function of the car, correlates this with and against the function of the house, and gains aspect and perspective as to their parents' real height; the representations will improve, becoming more 'refined' and 'true to life'. The child also begins to understand depth, and so will at some point move from drawing oblique two-dimensional pictures, to incorporating depth with 3 dimensional images. The perception of nuances in color, means that at around 16 years old, the child will possibly no longer paint a person as a sheet of brown, pink, white or yellow, but will begin to incorporate the tones which make up the complexion, creases, folds and shadows etc. Right now, the fullness of God is open to us, and if we pursue relationship, with time, our understanding, and therefore our representation of God, will improve. There is an issue if we do not move past the multi-colored blob stage, or even the *irrational* imagery where everything is the same size and two-dimensional.

It is interesting to consider that the fullness of God was present in The Garden of Eden with Adam, and Adam knew Him; yet Adam's understanding of God, did not give him insight into the nature of God enough, to know that when confronted with his sin, he could have called upon the name of Jesus, and repented! *Selah.*

Though Calvary had not yet happened in the time of this earth, God exists outside of time –salvation was there! Revelations 13:8 recounts the fact that The Lamb of God (Jesus) was slain <u>from the foundations of the world</u>. Adam had not moved past the juvenile multicolored blob understanding of God, and so even the fact that he sinned in the presence of God, is indicative that he did not fully know Father God, or understand the act of reverence of The Holy Spirit, or his all-knowing all present nature; let alone the redemptive power of Jesus.

> For as in Adam all die, even so in Christ
> shall all be made alive.
> [1 Corinthians 15:22]

Collectively and individually, we desperately need to raise our level of commitment, in love, in the lifestyle and pursuit of *knowing* God; moving past the juvenile, and as Paul stated in 1 Corinthians 13:11, put away childish things, *even childish understandings.* The fullness of God is truly open in the boundlessness of its rich depth and endlessness; freely and actively available to all who will receive Him.

At this juncture, I will add that in having a unified understanding of God as <u>ONE</u>, we can then begin to understand Him as seven – the seven spirits of God [Revelations 1:4, 3:1, 4:5, 5:6], which are seven representations or understandings of the <u>fullness of God</u> (One), as opposed to an additional seven which fit alongside the three. These seven 'personalities' (once understood) will only serve to enhance our unified understanding of God as <u>ONE</u>.

To walk in this understanding is the image of the mature adult; who identifies purpose in the process of balancing the entire image of their parents, so that within friendship, reverence, respect and honor are not lost. This is the mature adult who will STILL drop everything when their parent requires them, not out of fear or obligation, but out of love – for the greatest of these is LOVE. There is a tenderness of heart in this stage of relationship, which could be likened to that of a mother's love for her new born baby; love born out of something tangible – an undeniable bond, love with reckless abandon which declares itself true from her every fiber: to and for a being whose image and likeness is the same. Babies love passively, whereas a mother's love is active. It is a great testament to growth when a baby matures into an adult, and is able to actively *pour* that same mysterious depth of love, which he has cultivated within his heart for many decades, with sober, prehensile understanding, onto a mother who first loved him, unconditionally. *I pray that our aim would never deviate from knowing and loving God in this way.*

CHAPTER 3

FAITH, BELIEF, AND UNBELIEF

Jesus said unto him, If thou canst believe, all things are possible to him that believeth. [24]And straightway the father of the child cried out, and said with tears, Lord, I believe; help thou mine unbelief. [25]When Jesus saw that the people came running together, he rebuked the foul spirit, saying unto him, Thou dumb and deaf spirit, I charge thee, come out of him, and enter no more into him. [26]And the spirit cried, and rent him sore, and came out of him: and he was as one dead; insomuch that many said, He is dead. [27]But Jesus took him by the hand, and lifted him up; and he arose.

Mark 9:23-27
[KJV]

I am aware of the audacity of this title: faith, belief and unbelief are topics that could fill three entire volumes, let alone one chapter within a book; however, all three of these areas are ineluctably tied in symbiotic relationship with the heart, and so must be addressed within the confines of THC.

Faith

The Bible says that faith is the substance of things hoped for, the evidence of things not seen [Heb. 11:1]. Faith is therefore a form of knowledge, because knowledge is established upon evidence, which in turn substantiates its claim. Traditionally, 'knowledge' is conformed to the five senses, as it pertains to what can be seen, heard, tasted, smelled or touched/felt, whereas faith discerns the invisible and intangible. Faith is not hope – Faith is the confirmation, the guarantor; the substance of that which we hope for. Faith is not a 'feeling' – it is evidence, and as such, <u>faith is knowledge</u>. For this reason, faith enables you to make declarations, from a place of absolute knowing. "Blind faith" is therefore a misnomer, an oxymoron.

<u>Belief</u>

> "I think probably 90 percent of American
> people believe in the 10 commandments; [even though]
> 85 percent couldn't tell you what the 10 are..."
> -Supreme Court Justice Anton Scalia

Belief is a statement of where an individual stands on a matter. Many will attest, "I believe in God", yet the statement makes no commitment – that is the ambit of Faith. Belief is a basic understanding, or a respect/ honor toward a thing, without the need of comprehension. Unlike faith, belief stands alone – there is little to no evidence, yet we choose to believe.

be·lief *[bih-leef]*
noun

1 An acceptance that something exists or is true, especially one without proof.

2 Confidence in the truth or existence of something not immediately susceptible to rigorous proof

Belief will undergird, and activate faith. Jesus said:

> "22And Jesus answering saith unto them, Have **faith** in God.
> 23For verily I say unto you, That whosoever shall say unto this
> mountain, Be thou removed, and be thou cast into the sea; and
> shall **not doubt** in his heart, **but** shall **believe** that those things
> which he saith shall come to pass; he shall
> have whatsoever he saith.
> Mark 11:22-23

From this scripture, we can understand the mandate:

1. Have faith in God, and:
2. No doubt/ unbelief
3. Have belief

Unbelief

Many will miss the point of having no doubt, assuming that having no doubt is synonymous with having belief. It is not. Unbelief/ Doubt, exists as a separate entity - it is NOT just a description of the absence of belief, and can therefore coexist with belief. The opening scripture, Mark 9:24 demonstrates this: obviously the boy's father believed enough to bring his sick son to Jesus; however as much as he had belief, he also had unbelief.

Unbelief is the inverse of belief; that is to say, where belief and unbelief exist in equal measure, the net effect is zero. Unbelief is a particularly devastating aspect of THC, because of its silent and deadly nature. Unbelief will sit in the heart of an individual, with no symptoms, but will completely sterilize that person's faith, and belief.

Case study – Water Butts

Michael lives in a small East African village. He and his wife have 5 children. Back in December, Michael decided to purchase a water butt, knowing the rainy season was only a few months away (faith - the <u>evidence</u> of things not seen). Having such a big family, their water consumption is great, and so the rainy season presents a great opportunity for his family to store water, and a respite for his 2 daughters, who walk 5 miles every morning to fetch water before school. The rainy season comes, but the water butt isn't being filled – even in heavy downpours. Upon closer inspection, Michael realises that the water butt (belief) has several small holes in the sides. Unbelief is like the holes in the water butt, meaning that no matter how much rain comes, the barrel will always be empty. You can pray for more rain, but this won't solve the problem. You can get 3 more identical water butts, but again, this will not solve the problem. Until the issue of the holes is addressed, the holes (unbelief) will continue to undermine the integrity of the butt(s).

© The Heart Condition

Sometimes we get hung up on having more faith, but the reality is, we need very little faith – Jesus says with faith the size of a mustard seed, we can move a mountain [Mat. 17:12]. The issue many of us have is that even with faith and belief; many of us still sustain unbelief within our hearts. As illustrated above, even if you buy purchase 200 more water butts, but are still contending with unbelief, the increase of faith does nothing to alleviate the 'null' result.

SHOCK TACTICS

When you have faith in a thing and it doesn't happen, the obvious reaction is shock/ confusion. This is because faith IS evidence. Faith is the ability to look into the invisible and intangible, and see (through the eyes of the heart), and therefore KNOW that something specific is a reality. Howbeit then that when we supposedly have faith for something, and it happens, we also experience the shock and confusion? How many people believe God can raise the dead? How many people have faith in the fact that this is true? Honestly, how many people would be shocked and surprised if their recently deceased relative/ friend etc. was to get up from the funeral directors table.. honestly? If you answered yes to all three of those questions, I would like to congratulate you for your honesty; however what you have just identified is unbelief. If you go to the train station, you don't get surprised and confused when a train shows up at the advertised time – that's what you were expecting, and so clearly, when you pray for something and it happens, your subsequent shock is indicative of the fact that you were not actually expecting for it to happen. This shock is a mild example of the sterilizing effect of unbelief.

I remember a time that I was out with 2 friends. We were hanging out, and as we were talking, a group of homeless people came into the fast food restaurant we were in. We were led to pray for one of the ladies in the group, through a word of knowledge. After talking to her for a short time, she became surprisingly receptive and we began to minister. She broke down and truly opened her heart to a solution to her current state. We prayed with her for a while regarding her issues surrounding drug use, and for her children that had been taken into care, before eventually gaining the boldness to ask about the pair of crutches that were next to her. The lady explained that she had a condition called Osteomyelitis, (OSTY-OH-MY-UH-LIE-TUS) where the bone marrow is infected, causing a lot of pain to the sufferer. The condition also causes bone to soften, and so compresses under the weight of the body. This lady had 1 leg 6-8 inches shorter than the other, hence the crutches. We asked her if she wanted us to pray for healing, and she said yes. It was about 30 seconds into the prayer that she started to exclaim 'oh my God.. my leg.. I can feel it moving!' My hands were under her feet during the prayer, and so I actually had to readjust my position several times – there was no doubt about it – her leg was growing, right before our eyes as we prayed. After about 2 minutes, we asked her to stand up. Her right leg was now only about a cm shorter than her left leg. We prayed again, more fervently for complete healing. God healed the lady and we left after ministering God's Kingdom to a few others in the same fast food restaurant. As much as we walked away

48

with a feeling of victory, there was also a resounding sense of shock experienced by at least two out of the three of us, including myself.

We prayed to a God who heals, we prayed believing and with faith, but then when the inevitable happened I personally still manifested shock and amazement. Clearly, although I believed, and had faith, my 'shock' exposed the fact that there was still a small amount of unbelief in my heart; and although in this instance, it had not hindered this woman's healing, it got me thinking – what else would God have had us do, were it not for the unbelief present in our hearts? Don't get me wrong – this was not about beating myself up, or feeling guilty, but truly; how much good is negated, even in daily life, because of unbelief? This is a very worthy contemplation; toward the goal of total submission into God's word – even in our systems of (un)belief.

This was an example of when I'd actually been sensitive enough to (retroactively) detect my unbelief, but now with hindsight, I have to consider: how many times have I prayed about a situation; personal or otherwise, and no sooner than the prayer left my heart, undermined my own prayer with my unbelief?

There are testimonies we share about God's greatness, which are not actually testimonies of God's greatness, but something which our unbelief has told us are. Case in point - It is not God's will to partially heal somebody – this isn't a New Covenant concept found anywhere in scripture. NOWHERE. Why then do we rejoice so vehemently when we see this happen? Yes, we rejoice in all things, but if God has made a promise, then why do we try to 'excuse' ourselves from the expectation of seeing it made manifest? This is a fruit of unbelief: a supine, weak willed imitation of belief; having a vague resemblance to Godliness, but denying its power [2 Timothy 3:5].

Even thinking back to my experience of the homeless lady who was healed from Osteomyelitis – honestly, looking back, I do not remember being released from her. We had decided amongst ourselves that it was time to go home; slightly tired, and with an overriding, overinflated sense of accomplishment. As previously mentioned, this lady actually opened her heart to the possibility of a solution to her condition – the solution was sozo; not just healing. The reality is, whilst we spoke about Jesus and His sozo, this lady had truly only experienced 1/3. Inebriated by a toxic cocktail of accomplishment and unbelief, we 'sat on our laurels'; contenting ourselves with a rough charcoal outline sketch, when what God had intended was a fine art painted masterpiece. This woman walked away healed in her body, but still bound in chains. Selah.

LORD, I believe, yet help my unbelief.

... BY PRAYER AND FASTING

¹⁹Then came the disciples to Jesus apart, and said, Why could not we cast him out? ²⁰And Jesus said unto them, **Because of your unbelief**: for verily I say unto you, If ye have faith as a grain of mustard seed, ye shall say unto this mountain, Remove hence to yonder place; and it shall remove; and nothing shall be impossible unto you. ²¹**Howbeit this kind goeth not out but by prayer and fasting**.
Matthew 17:19-22
[KJV]

The above scripture has been grossly misunderstood, and therefore misrepresented in Christendom today; especially prevalent in modern Pentecostal theology. This has resulted in a belief, that some rankings of demons require prayer and fasting to be cast be cast out. This is a <u>false doctrine</u>. Only faith in the power of the name of Jesus can cast a demon out – if Jesus cannot cast a demon out (impossible), then fasting and prayer would not be of any extra assistance to you. If you re-read Matthew 17:19-22, what is being talked about here is **unbelief**. *'Howbeit this kind goeth not out by prayer and fasting'*, refers to the disciples' unbelief, <u>which Jesus says is responsible for them not being able to cast a demon out</u> (verse 20). Prayer and fasting casts out unbelief – not demons.

Hunger is one appetite which is undeniably common to man – you can abstain from many things, but fasting as it pertains to abstinence from food (and water if dry fasting), is a very direct, deliberate and extremely effective way to re-establish divine order in our whole man – a spirit, yielded to God, which informs the soul, via the heart, and a soul which instructs the flesh in righteousness. Doubt or "unbelief" is cast out in this model, as there simply is no room for it.

When we decide in our heart to fast, what we are actually doing is declaring internal warfare, <u>which is the act of STANDING to see the will of God established</u>. In cutting off nutritional stimulation, the flesh grumbles to the soul. Instead of comforting the flesh in the fact that <u>it is not food, but God which sustains life</u>; a renegade, poorly disciplined soul brings this complaint, with lamentation to the heart - this is why many people manifest *emotional* imbalance during periods of fasting such as anger, tears, irritability and short-temperedness. The individual who is able to STAND whilst fasting (prayer helps this, by sharpening our spirit), will silence the pangs of the soul – a silenced soul, which will now receive instruction from the spirit.

During fasting, we educate the soul to knowing that it has the propensity toward being reactionary, and train it in the knowledge that it is only under the tutelage of the spirit - a spirit yielded to God, through Christ, that it will ever find peace. Every single question the soul asks is fully resolved when it eventually grasps this revelation, and in the assimilation of this knowledge, the soul no longer tries to 'manage up', but now takes the revelation, and 'manages down', training the flesh. In this way, discipline is trained into the 'whole man', from the spirit down.

Want to cast out unbelief, and sharpen your spirit? Make fasting (with prayer) an integral part of your worship lifestyle.

<u>SIN</u>

I acknowledged my **sin** to you and did not cover up my **iniquity**.
I said, 'I will confess my **transgressions** to the LORD
-Psalm 32:5

Again, I will start by saying; this topic is indeed immense. However, the topic of sin is a very important concept to touch upon when it comes to THC - especially when we consider that the decision and/or ability to refrain from sin, is the remit of your heart [Psalm 119:11]. We use the word 'sin' in a very broad sense – a term which covers a number of acts/ behaviors; however The Bible differentiates these 'behaviors' into three specific groups:

> <u>Sin</u> is the act of not hitting the mark
> <u>Transgression/ Trespass</u> is the act of crossing the line
> <u>Iniquity</u> is the habit or lifestyle of soiling the soul.
> -Pastor Tope Koleoso – Jubilee Church, UK

For the sake of clarity, both transgression and iniquity are theoretically, by definition, types of '*sin*', because both of them require us to 'miss the mark', and do something outside of the will of God, and so when I refer to '*sin*' as opposed to sin, I am referring to the broader group of behavior (including transgression and iniquity).

To take a slight Segway, I think it's important to establish the fact that through Christ; because of Calvary, sins, transgressions and iniquity; '*sins*', are removed from us [1 Peter 3:18, Isaiah 53:5, 1Cor 15:1-4]. The Bible says, even of transgressions that, 'as far as the east is from the west, so far hath he removed our transgressions from us' [Psalm 103:12], and so with this, understand that there is given an implicit responsibility to sustain said distance. Christ and Calvary, grace and mercy are <u>not</u> justifications, or 'hall passes' for '*sin*', but deliverance from The Kingdom of darkness into The

Kingdom of Light comes, enabling and supporting the elimination of **all** delinquent behaviors – for good.

We have conditioned our hearts into accepting that *sin* is a viable way to live; <u>a lifestyle of "missing the mark"</u>, some popular statements of faith being 'after all, we're not perfect', and 'I'm a work in progress' (yet there has been no progress in over 5 years). Even in the absence of transgression or iniquity, because of sin, our hearts present a false reality to our minds' comprehension of The Word of God.

Your beliefs don't make you a better person;
Your behavior does.....

Matthew 5:48 states 'Be ye <u>perfect</u>, even as your Father which is in heaven is <u>perfect</u>'. 1 Peter 1:16 echoes the same sentiment – be ye holy, for I AM holy. This means that in spite of what you have experienced in life, no matter what you have been misinformed into believing regarding your '*sin*', such as, "even righteous men struggle with something" or, "nobody can be perfect"; there is a reasonable, truthful, and realistic (because it came from an all knowing, all wise God) expectation for you and I to be exactly that - <u>perfect</u>. All have sinned and fallen short, but 'now that you are in Christ, I want you to be perfect; never missing the mark again'. Truly, the individual who makes God their habitation, who 'hides' God in their heart, and whose heart is purposely turned toward Him continually, will NOT miss the mark. "Thy word have I hid in mine heart, that I might not sin against thee". In layman's terms, if you plant potatoes, it is **impossible** to reap tulips. If you have allowed God an habitation within you, this will be evidenced by your fruit, and '*sin*' is not a fruit of this Kingdom.

The issue with '*sin*' is that it is not only an action, but that over time, it will malform and disfigure our ability to process the truth of God – especially when it comes to iniquity. 'Sin' is not just an act, but also a <u>conditioning process</u>. For most people, it is so embedded in their being, or their heart is so conditioned toward it, that they cannot reconcile the word 'perfect' and their concept of the will of God for their life, right now. This is a big issue. Not only is this a gross underestimation of God and His ability to change a life, but it is a dictionary-precise example of idolatry; when you exalt something else above God - even an opinion concerning what is feasible, possible and realistic for your life. Calvary's ability to remove 'sin' is extended to all – the righteous, and the unrighteous alike, but the goal is for you and I to find our footing in God (and keep it); unwavering, resilient and righteous - Holy. We comprehend that a touch from 'sin', or 'evil' *can* dramatically change a life forever – consider rape, or gun crime; but somehow in our hearts we have believed a lie (THC) when it comes to comprehending the fact that a touch from God WILL change a life forever, for the good, to a degree and intensity that 'sin', evil or the devil never could. Now consider God – the infinite splendor and majesty of power and perfection, in love, giving His life to birth you, through sozo, into His Kingdom; and what this means, as a result in direct application to your life.

For the [true] love of God is this: that we do His commands [keep His ordinances and are mindful of His precepts and teaching]. And these orders of His are not irksome (burdensome, oppressive, or grievous).

1 John 5:3[AMP]

Lord, create in me a PURE heart. Re-inform my systems of belief, and condition me; receptive to the truth and reality of what and whom you desire me to be.

CHAPTER 4

THC – THE MASTER INEBRIANT

Very early on in the day, when God began to speak to me about The Heart Condition, He bought me to the realization that the effects of THC upon an individual are almost identical to that of a perception altering narcotic, and more specifically, that of the Cannabinoid of the same name, *Tetrahydrocannabinol* THC ($_{THC}^{1}$ for the sake of differentiation). For those of you left blank-faced at that last statement, $_{THC}^{1}$ is the chemical component of interest in the cannabis plant, i.e. when we talk about cannabis as a drug; weed, hash, punk, skunk, sensi, marijuana, these all derive their potency from their concentration of the $_{THC}^{1}$ compound. I hasten to establish, that this chapter is *not* about trying to extol the evils and dangers of drugs - there is a vast array of literature out there for that purpose. In this chapter, comparisons are simply being drawn; highlighting the similarities between the (purported) effects of the $_{THC}^{1}$ in cannabis upon an individual, vs the effects of THC; and exploring what can be learned from these observations.

$_{THC}^{1}$ is a compound with some amazing physiological actions, which has kept it as the subject of medical research science for over 50 years. $_{THC}^{1}$ is a powerful substance, and so without proper regulation, what *could* have been a great assistance to an individual, could very quickly become dangerous. $_{THC}{}^1$ is known to impair cognitive and motor skills, cause emotional and sometimes psychological imbalance in an individual, and is also a calmative; the go to substance for those who want something to 'get by'. Throughout time, many *considered* great artists, musicians, philosophers etc., have used cannabis, and considered it their muse, possibly due to its psychoactive, perception altering properties.

The human heart, (as it pertains to the part soul, part spirit mediator/conduit between the soul and the spirit) is an amazing and powerful thing. Under proper stewardship, a conditioned heart will sustain and modulate, a peaceful and harmonious life; however without proper regulation we see a dangerous and malignant manifestation of THC. It is a dysfunctional behavior, which arose to help an individual to 'get by', but actually ends up causing more harm, than any of the temporary good it may have been perceived to have done. People who sit in seats of excellence, even in our churches, are rich case studies for THC, and if we were to run a *blood test* to 'discern' these individuals' heart condition there would almost certainly be a disproportionately high number of positive results.

Cannabis has been used throughout the ages as a medicine, a psycho-spiritual stimulant by shamans, '*holy men*', and witches, and as fragrant incense. Because of its pungent earthy-sweet aroma, it was known as 'Sweet Calamus/ Keneh Bosem', and we even see its use in Exodus 30:22-33, where it can be found as one of the five ingredients of the Holy Anointing Oil.

The naturally occurring $_{THC}{}^1$ in cannabis is what causes it to be classified as a narcotic; a mind, perception, and behavior altering controlled or illegal substance. It is also what you would call an inebriant, meaning a substance which silences the world, and releases an individual into a state of *apparent* bliss; completely unaware of his/her surroundings. In this sense, $_{THC}{}^1$ 'dumbs down' sensory information, meaning that although ten people in a room are experiencing the same thing, the person under the influence of $_{THC}{}^1$ will have a <u>compromised understanding of what he/she has</u>

experienced. It is this property of $_{THC}^{1}$ which makes it a superior painkiller, or *analgesic*.

NUMBING THE PAIN

Individuals who contend with a debilitating and painful condition and experience little to no relief from taking pharmaceutical painkillers, report a dramatic decrease in the perception of that pain whilst self-medicating with $_{THC}^{1}$ in the form of cannabis, skunk or hash. $_{THC}^{1}$ numbs the pain, and so many defend its use. The problem with constantly blocking pain, is that pain is a messaging system, which ultimately informs the brain, that something is wrong somewhere in the body. Blocking the pain does not alleviate the problem, and doing so, over a period of time, only causes the body to produce more pain mediators because you don't seem to be addressing the problem. It also opens the individual up to making silly decisions, which could be very damaging to his/her health. An illustration is an individual with crippling arthritic joint pain: painkillers are prescribed, and within days that person is able to walk and manipulate their joints as normal – but the problem still remains: the joints. Because the individual can't feel the pain, they are unaware that when they are now able to walk, pain free, the weight of their body is further crumbling their joints to pieces with every step. Over time, the individual will have to increase their pain medication, as the body intensifies its release of pain mediators in an attempt to make the individual stop, change their habits, and address the underlying issue.

Pain is a horrible thing to contend with – I mean real unceasing, unthinkably crippling pain, that most of us will thankfully never endure, is a daily reality for some, that will have an individual writhing on the floor in agony, on insanity's cusp; *but* the reality is that pain is there to tell us something for our own good. If we block the pain, but don't sort out the issue that caused the pain in the first place, we are essentially switching off the light to avoid dealing with the infestation of elephants in the room.

THC[1] is a master at not only numbing the pain, but also altering mindsets, and causing delusions. This is an extremely dangerous combination – it is one thing to be pain free, but to be simultaneously in a deluded, altered state of mind is always going to be a recipe for disaster. Going back to the previous example, the individual self-medicates with THC[1], and so now not only is she able to get back to her normal schedule, but with the delusion, she feels so great, that she decides to take up jogging - big mistake! The damage caused by THC[1] is not, for the most part, direct damage from the drug, but from the flawed perception it gives the user, and what they subsequently end up doing (or not) as a result.

There is a condition called *Congenital Insensitivity to Pain*. If you ever have a chance to look into it, you will find horrific pictures of babies who have bitten off their tongue; children with missing fingers; people with horrific burns all over their body, especially hands, after lifting hot pans and dishes without gloves; corneal abrasions where eyes have been rubbed to the point of damage – these are all examples of what happen when you cannot feel pain. Babies born without this sensation will very easily bite off fingers and toes without any understanding of the negative consequences of the action. Similarly, both THC[1] and THC numb the pain and can subsequently cause an individual to do hurtful and damaging things; things which they would never do had they been in their 'right mind'. Pain is a very valuable teacher, and stops us from causing further hurt to ourselves; re-evaluating the implication of what we were doing which caused the pain to come, opening the door for change.

In a major international study, published in *The Lancet* on Thursday 30th May 2013, the chronic use of painkillers was linked to an increased risk of heart attack (MI) by one third. This is <u>exactly</u> what happens with THC, a system which constantly blocks pain; the heart will gradually weaken, and eventually fail.

HYPERDIMENSIONAL INTERACTIONS

The word hyperdimensional simply refers to interactions outside of the three perceivable dimensions of this reality; breadth/ length, depth and height. Cannabis has been used for thousands of years in mysticism and religious rituals, to elucidate altered states of mind, trances and out of body experiences. Cannabis is broadly known as a 'gateway drug', because people often graduate from Cannabis to 'harder drugs' such as cocaine, but from a spiritual sense, Cannabis truly is a gateway drug. One of its touted *benefits* is its ability to 'open the heart', which in turn is said to transport the individual to other realms of reality. The 'hallucinations' that a small handful of people will sometimes suffer under the influence of $_{THC}{}^1$, are actually not always hallucinations, but because the heart has opened; the five non-physical senses of the heart can be prematurely activated, such as sight, or 'the eyes of the heart', as mentioned in Ephesians 1:1. The user can now see into a previously invisible realm, and understandably, for most, this is an extremely traumatic and disturbing experience. Now, The Bible says in Proverbs 4:23 that we should above all else, guard our hearts, yet $_{THC}{}^1$ opens the heart, indiscriminately, meaning that:

- The heart is open to emotional residue, *ambient* information, and beings.
- Aspects of a person's internal makeup, are now exposed, and will react with external forces, often without the person's knowledge.
- A chasm is created, disconnecting the spirit and the soul.

Because of the vacuum that now exists between the spirit and the soul, the soul can now operate completely independently of the spirit. This is another expression of inebriation. Because of the chasm, the spirit can now leave the body in what occultists call astral travel, astral projection, or remote viewing (or be encouraged out of by another spirit). Because the heart gate is very definitely open, all manner of spirits now have a clear channel to minister to the soul, whether or not the spirit has left. Occultists would call this channeling.

In THC, the heart may be hardened against specific things – like a person's bad experiences. However generally speaking, the heart is unguarded, because only the understanding of The Word of God applied to a willing life, can effectively guard, or 'keep' a heart. Although THC doesn't necessarily cause out of body phenomena, it *will* cause an individual to feel distant, not themselves, and wanting to 'return to themselves'.

Manifestations from $_{THC}{}^1$ include depression, schizophrenia and bipolar tendencies, which can also be found manifested in THC. Another aspect of this is that when one uses $_{THC}{}^1$, the mind can 'slip' past the 3rd dimension, into the dimension of time - this is interesting, because although the individual is now insensitive to time, and so time seems to be moving slower, or indeed, to be standing still, time continues as normal in the *real world*. These individuals will often just 'lose' ten years, spent in mediocrity, with little to no movement in their lives.

THC similarly, will cause an individual to be on a continuous loop of 'waking sleep'; having a faint grasp on reality – an unfortunate daydream, whilst life continues in the background. Unless TRUE reality, as laid out in The Word of God, is the only reality manifest in our lives, we desperately need to address where the reality we are currently sitting in, came from.

It is time to wake up.

CHAPTER 5

MYOCARDIAL INFACTION – ATTACK OF THE HEART

A sound heart is the life of the flesh: but envy the rottenness of the bones.
Proverbs 14:30
[KJV]

The medical term myocardial infarction (MI) refers to the death of (infarction) muscle (myo-) tissue, caused by oxygen deprivation, due to an interruption in the blood flow to the heart (cardial); in short, a heart attack. MI is usually caused by some form of blockage, which results in a temporary stop to the heart's blood supply, thus preventing the delivery of oxygen to the cells and inducing necrosis (cell death). Similarly, the individual under the influence of THC, will at times, find the inner pathways of their heart blocked, Christ (The blood), shut out, which in turn blocks the Holy Spirit (air/ oxygen) from entering in to nourish and sustain us, thus causing us to experience discomfort, and a form of death. The icon of MI is a perfect example, demonstrating to us how important the blood (Christ) is to our health, and when we are shut off from the blood, even temporarily, how devastating the results are.

Generally, as Sons and Daughters, this is no great revelation - we get this, and we aim to live our lives in a way that is conducive to sustaining blood flow; however, please understand and do not be ignorant to the capacity of THC to impair one's ability to competently perceive. In MI, the heart is temporarily disengaged – completely shut down. This causes lapsed judgment, therefore further compromising the decision making process and promotes poor shepherding of *free will*.

THC, at its heart is deception; especially when it comes to matters of the spirit. By this, I am not for a minute suggesting that one's spiritual "aptitude" is a marker by which you can discern whether or not that individual is bound by THC. Spiritual gifts are given, are not revoked, and they make no apology for themselves [Romans 11:29]. Have you ever witnessed a great man or woman of God, great in the gifts of the spirit, but just MEAN hearted? Someone who could preach down a mountain, but behind closed doors is a fornicator and an adulterer? These examples are rich case studies of individuals who, though great, contend with THC. I have seen Pastors; Prophets; individuals with immense healing gifts, and gifts for breakthrough and deliverance who suffered from THC. That statement is in no way made to attack or defame the established body of Christ, but to encourage an understanding, in maturity, of exactly how deep and yet subtle this condition really is. Diagnosis is the first step to recovery - if everyone who reads this book identifies THC as something that 'other people' have, then these words are in vain.

Those under its influence will regularly encounter MI, and as "good Christians" remain perplexed as to why their lives manifest as though they weren't even saved. THC won't necessarily send you to hell, but it will definitely manifest a kind of hell into your life. This is totally unnecessary, and NOT a part of God's will or promise to us, whom He calls *beloved*.

DISENGAGING THE HEART

Within MI, the heart is temporarily disengaged, and that is exactly what happens in THC. With reference back to the diagram on page 5, a disengaged heart means that the soul is no longer under the tutelage of the spirit, and is therefore free to do as it pleases. In this, we can see how MI is sometimes self-inflicted; a desirable option toward the outcome of a disengaged heart. Imagine a strong soulish desire which is subdued by the spirit, through the conduit of the heart. This is problematic, because when the desire is only subdued and not removed; it is only a matter of time before this 'slumbering lion' wakes up, more irate than when it was put to sleep.

When the desire intensifies, the individual can either cause that desire to become lodged in the heart, thus causing MI, OR the soul and its desires can intentionally suffocate the heart into submission, to the point of disengaging. 'Hardening' ones heart is a description of exactly this. This is a convenient way used by many to 'get over' that first step into sin. Without 'the court of God' in operation, there is no conviction, and so the individual is free to do as he or she pleases *without feeling judged*.

Sin is so much easier with a disengaged heart, which almost acts as a permit for actions based out of (to name but a few); fear, anger, unforgiveness and lust.

There's an old saying:

> *'Holding a grudge against someone is like drinking*
> *poison and expecting the other person to die'.*

This is yet another problem with disengaging the heart. Not only are you purposely preparing yourself for sin, but disengaging the heart, cuts you off from 'the blood supply'. You disengaged your heart to act in a way which your felt was beneficial, yet in actuality, the opposite is true. In a practical sense, this means that everything your spirit knows about your worth - everything which The Holy

Spirit and scripture could ever minister to you about who you are, in Christ, is lost. Disengaging throws open the door to insecurity, and so people with disengaged hearts often display this through outlets such as the caliber of 'friends' they keep, the quality of interactions/relations, patterns of 'permissive abuse', promiscuity, an over-compensating demeanor, subservient behavior and low self-esteem.

People often disengage their hearts in order to seek 'comfort', to seek refuge or as a means of escape – especially within the Kingdom, where we have the revelation of grace, mercy and the atonement of sin… boldly acting in a way that is contrary to the way we know we should, under the all atoning *internal excuse*, that, 'Well, I'm *sorta* allowed to… Jesus paid it – and it's just temporary…' No different from the individual on a diet with a weakness for chocolate, a weak will, and a bag of excuses, which prevent them from ever losing any weight.

Have you ever witnessed a child crying because their parent prevents them from partaking in something which would be harmful to them? Think of a small, brightly colored, shiny marble that a baby wants to swallow, but the parent knowing better prevents this from happening – this is what the informed heart does to the soul. The baby cannot comprehend that this isn't an appropriate desire, and unless the parent is able to effectively teach that child, he or she will no doubt one day swallow a marble. The reality is, that marble will *never* be able to offer that child what he or she had desired from that experience – clearly the parent had judged this and so acted to prevent it. However, this is the folly we go though every time we disengage our heart.

The desires, the grudges, the opinions you disengage your heart for – even temporarily, will never give you the 'comfort' or the 'escape' you were looking for. How can voluntary bondage offer escape? How can there ever be comfort, by cutting off ministration from THE Comforter, The Holy Spirit? Whether the reason you disengage your heart is in order to indulge in a bad attitude, inappropriate conversation, gossip, fornication, anger, envy, pride, egotism… murder - none of these have the capability to bless, to build, to comfort or to bestow liberty – there is <u>never</u> a <u>true</u> reason to disengage ones heart.

Holy Spirit, expose to me the areas in which I disengage my heart. Help me to break this useless habit, so that I can truly engage my heart in all that I say, think and do – to your Glory. Amen.

<u>OBSTRUCTION – THE MILK DIET</u>

When looking at obstruction of the physical heart, as it pertains to MI, an interesting consideration is the build-up of arterial plaque, due to the over consumption of dairy products. This plaque not only affects the heart, but also can also impair brain function, and has recently been linked to conditions such as stroke and Alzheimer's disease. It has also been linked to erectile dysfunction and impotence, and truly - as a Child of God, if you stay on a milk diet for too long, you will end up confused, and infertile; unable to pinpoint, discern or bring forth the things which have already been deposited within you, by God. I would comfortably hypothesize that the majority of the body is still on a 100% milk diet [1 Cor 3:2; Heb. 5:12], and have not yet progressed to solid food. In and of itself, this is not actually an issue if this is where they need to be – you eat at your level, until you are ready to progress, and in truth, milk is still nourishment. The issue however is that in THC, because individuals find it hard to digest whole truth, the milk is only part digested, where it sits within their comprehension and stagnates. This is essentially how arterial plaque is formed; when partially digested food, and non-expelled waste accumulate and form a strange cement-like substance. This process is exactly how some of our theology, individually and collectively, has been formed, in The Kingdom.

The solution therefore, is not to start eating meat – this would only further aggravate the situation. The individual who has not learned to fully digest, process and utilize *milk*, is going to have even more issues when it comes to the digestion of *meat*. The only remedy therefore, would be to go back to the beginning – Invite the Holy Spirit to remove the plaque, and to lay down the foundations of a comprehensive digestive system, which is able to break down and subsequently reconstitute rich sustenance from what we consume, throughout the body. In this model, we appreciate the varied depth of nutrition in what we consume, and nothing goes to waste, which leaves our innermost pathways open and **clean** for *The Blood* to flow freely to (and from) our hearts.

BARE BONES

Biblically, bones have always represented structure, fortitude, integrity, truth and right standing. The way God has formed us further echoes this truth; that with all the integrity, structure and right standing in the world (bones) - without muscle, those qualities (bones) cannot, and will not move, but will instead become parched and dry, or stagnant and rotten. Not only that, but muscle provides the first instance whereby all these qualities are bound together: muscle secures, and keeps the bone correctly orientated. MI causes muscle paralysis and muscle death, and can lead to stroke. This will subsequently prevent further bone use, for a period of time. Whether arms or legs, no matter how strong they may be, MI has the power to immobilize you, and can in turn, cause dis-locatcation, and bad posture. The spiritual mirror of that, is: faith (muscle) is the vehicle, the means by which you, even in the fortitude of your holiness, will be transported to the place that God has desired for you. When faith becomes slack, it will change the posture of your heart. Without faith, it is impossible to please God, and I say this, contrasted against the background of THC, and the many complications it encapsulates; including MI, which will smother and suffocate your faith, by temporarily cutting off the blood supply. As believers, we all know we have faith, but please remember the ability that THC has to undermine that faith with unbelief. And when faith is dead, EVERYTHING goes on hold... Destiny.. Purpose - everything. I want you to understand that the action of THC is extremely subtle - it can slip below the radar of even the most "pious" Christian, because *THC isn't actually sin.* THC is a subtle condition which affects the silent inner workings of the heart, and can suddenly strike, paralyzing without warning, thus causing us to miss the mark.

In THC, the soul is made fat in its obstinacy, where it dominates and *literally* crushes the spirit into submission. The Bible says that a crushed spirit dries up the bones [Pro 17:22]. Through this scripture, we can see how THC, which would mis-orientate the soul, crushing the spirit, WOULD indeed dry up the bones, leaching all the goodness, until the bones become brittle, making it hard to *stand* - THC is not sin, but it will make your walk painful. Selah. An ex-lover, a behavior, an addiction or habit - all these things can become lodged in the unguarded heart, where they will eventually become a blockage, resulting in MI.

*Above **all** else guard your heart, because from it flows the springs of life.* [Proverbs 4:23]

CHAPTER 6

EMPATHY

"The light of the eyes rejoiceth the heart: and a
good report maketh the bones fat."
Proverbs 15:30
[KJV]

empathy [ˈɛmpəθɪ]

The power of understanding and imaginatively entering into another person's personality, and experiencing his feelings.

Webster's dictionary puts it like this:

"The action of understanding, being aware of, being sensitive to, and *vicariously* experiencing the feelings, thoughts, and experience of another of either the past or present without having the feelings, thoughts, and experience fully communicated in an objectively explicit manner."

Empathy is the ability of an individual, most often through personal experience, to walk into another person's situation, experience it, and therefore have a heartfelt understanding of that particular situation. The ability to empathize is usually reserved for those who have had prior experience in that specific area. The most someone who hasn't had that experience can usually offer

68

is sympathy. Sympathy is a surface feeling of regret, at another's circumstances.

Over the next two chapters we will look at the world's model of empathy, and its ability to undermine The Word of God, juxtaposed against compassion; God's design for every Christian. And how, through compassion revolutionary change, salvation, healing and deliverance [sozo] are ordered.

THE PROBLEM WITH EMPATHY

Keep thy heart with all diligence; for out of it flow the issues of life.
Proverbs 4:23
[KJV]

For as a man thinketh in his heart, so is he...
Proverbs 23:7-8
[KJV]

Finally, brethren, whatsoever things are true, whatsoever things [are] honest, whatsoever things [are] just, whatsoever things [are] pure, whatsoever things [are] lovely, whatsoever things [are] of good report; if [there be] any virtue, and if [there be] any praise, think on these things.
Philippians 4:8
[AMP]

I want to start this section by saying that I truly believe empathy is a dysfunctional behavior; a fruit of THC, whose seed is perennial, i.e. empathy will continue to re-cultivate every 'feeling/seed' in its repertoire for as long as empathy is entertained within the heart of the individual. I would like to describe the act of empathy as engaging one's heart in intercourse with another individual's infected heart, which in turn corrupts and causes a systemic malfunction in the heart of the individual expressing empathy. Whilst empathy may (or may not) assist an individual in a difficult situation, please understand that the act of empathy requires you to disregard the three scriptures above, and of course, every time we close out the word of God in favor of a 'feeling', calamity follows. In terms of the specific heart condition, this is no different to the act of fornication; ignoring the word of God, because of a "feeling".

On the surface, empathy is what the caring person does - my Grandmother always used to say, 'He who feels it, knows it'; and this is true. It is the most obvious statement in the world to say that the individual, who has for example successfully given up smoking cigarettes, is going to be most understanding/ sensitive/ empathetic toward the person who is two weeks into trying to quit. On the surface, this looks like a positive thing: especially when it comes to ministry. If there is an individual who comes from a specific past, and the minister can empathize because of shared experience, then surely, said minister; whilst being sensitive to that person's needs and requirements, will be able to best plot out the nuances of that particular individual's road to salvation. Now of this stance, I would say the following:

- Jesus IS the road to salvation. All who call upon His name will be saved. He IS the way, the truth, the door and the light. His word is a lamp unto our path and a light unto our feet – no further illumination is required.

- We know in part, we prophesy in part – experience, whether individual or collective can never teach us everything we need to know. What He teaches is always going to be deeper, richer and more poignant than what your experience has taught. Period.

- Empathy is like a lubricant which impedes one's ability to stand flat-footed on God's Word as a conduit of His love, ushering in peace, but will instead encourage 'strange' wisdom to flow from the lips of one's emotion, with detrimental effect to both the orator and the recipient(s).

- In spite of the depth of turmoil you may have experienced in your past, it is **impossible** that you have more love or compassion in your heart than Jesus, at any given time.

Therefore any strategy born out of empathy, which makes 'allowances' for a person's past or present situation, relative to God's requirements for <u>all</u> of mankind, implicitly suggests that God committed an oversight, and is therefore flawed.

EXPERIENCE - THE DEFENSE FOR EMPATHY

Let us discuss experience for a moment. No one comes into this world 'saved'. The Bible says that all have sinned and fallen short of the glory of God – EVERYONE has had experience outside of The Kingdom. Yet, I put it to you that God did not require any of us to go through what we went through in order to come to the realization that we stand in today – no matter how pivotal that moment was in your life. <u>There is nothing The Kingdom of Darkness can offer in establishing The Kingdom of God</u> – it is insulting to suggest this. Trying to insist that The Kingdom of God is more equipped, or in some way better off because some of its members tarried in The Kingdom of Darkness, and gained 'experience', 'knowledge' and/or 'wisdom', is a ridiculous stance to take, when we serve a God who created all things, knows all things, and is everywhere; simultaneously.

Yes, for some of us - including myself, folly and calamity had to come, because of stubbornness - stubbornness to what? To God's will and word, which came in part to teach and to edify. The world will tell you that experience is the best teacher, but your Bible says it's The Holy Spirit. Who do you believe? It's wonderful that we have triumphed over our past, learned some amazing lessons, been established in our faith, and have walked into tomorrow holding the hand of King Jesus. However, the experience of sin doesn't qualify us for salvation, [sozo] or the promise of The Kingdom - Jesus does. One of my favorite statements –cliché, but very true: God doesn't call the qualified – He qualifies the called. That is to say that though your experience, may have qualified you in the specific area of your calling, the fact is that you were called before you were qualified - before conception; and so at the point that you answered that call (even though without qualification), God enables you to become qualified, through His Spirit, eg: the ex-drug dealer, who is now able to minister to incarcerated drug dealers, vs. the young man who has never dealt drugs, who is still able to minister to the drug dealers, <u>at an equal or greater level</u>, because of the anointing and therefore qualification of God upon his life. The fact is, that even with experience, when you come into The Kingdom, you *still* need to come under submission to The Word of God. Your 'qualification' means nothing, because *your 'qualified opinions' are not what save.*

The reality is that THC has us, even in churches, fixated on how 'qualified' a person is for a specific task, using the five senses of man, instead of the word of God: what does God say? King David (a boy, yet King of Israel) comes to mind. And I know many might say, 'well he was a shepherd, and shepherds have the qualities that are desirable in a king, such as stewardship and compassion for every single member of his flock', and I would agree – these are desirable qualities, but what is being described is a list of transferable skills – not qualification. Skills in animal husbandry, do not a King make. Samuel, the 'super prophet', even with the keenness of his eyes, could not see past this.

When we carry something out of our past and try to use it to bring hope or effect change in our present/ future, we mess up. No matter how valuable that thing appears to be, God says: I have something better for you – leave it <u>all</u> behind. There are many instances in scripture where God has required individuals to 'kill everything', or 'take nothing'. Why? Because otherwise we fixate on the ability of 'that thing' to assist us in some way shape or form, to the point that we unwittingly close out God, and become involved in idolatry. THC will open you up to confusion from the secular standards of the day, when the truth is that God does not require experience or opinions, but <u>obedience</u>. Seek ye first The Kingdom of God, and all else will be added unto you - even information and wisdom BEYOND experience.

THE HEART MURMUR

The healthy, aligned human heart, beats to a very specific rhythm - the sound created by this rhythm is described as lub-DUPP" or "lub-DUB". A Heart Murmur (HM) will manifest as an extra or *unusual* sound heard during a heartbeat. There is often a very obvious cause of the extra sound, such as valve damage; however when there is no obvious cause, the HM is classified as "innocent". This is when the medical professional can see no reason why the heart would be making extra noises, as it *appears* to be 'healthy'. The reality is, "innocent" HM's are (in my opinion), poorly named, as evidenced by the anomalous and deviant sound. The "innocent" condition *can* be far more devastating, and due to its subtle nature; unexpected, if/ when a secondary issue develops. What's even more interesting about this condition is that sometimes HM is congenital, i.e. it exists from the time of birth. If the HM is deemed to be "innocent", little to no intervention will be attempted to correct a seemingly "non-existent" problem. This individual will then go on to live a seemingly 'healthy' life, with a heart whose sound is flawed. The sound of a physical heart beat is generated by oxygenated blood, traveling through the chambers of the heart, and amplified relative to its structure. To the trained ear, this sound can be transliterated into a three dimensional schematic diagram of the heart, giving insight into the capacities, traumas and health of the heart. In this manner, the heart can be described as a *high instrument.*

The spiritual equivalent of 'innocent' HM, is the individual who is saved, and lives a holy life, YET there is sound which emanates from their heart, which doesn't quite match up. Another expression of sound is 'resonance'. HM will mean that although holiness is found within you, and therefore you will resonate holiness, it will be tainted with something unusual - think of an inharmonious or muffled sound. This strange sound is so subtle, yet will permeate and affect every aspect of an individual's being. Whereas worship should produce a sweet and pure fragrance, HM will taint it with a damp and musty undertone. The 'high instrument' of worship is, in part, turned away from God.

In this light, the HM could be a generational belief or false honor system, anxiety, fear, arrogance, pride, superstition – things which should really not be found in a Christian.

Is the sound of your heart PURE?

Lord, let my heart beat to your rhythm - synchronous; harmonious; aligned.

EXITING SODOM

A well-known Bible story is that of Lot's exit from Sodom:

> And it came to pass, when they had brought them forth abroad, that he said, Escape for thy life; look not behind thee, neither stay thou in all the plain; escape to the mountain, lest thou be consumed.
> **Genesis 19:17**
> [KJV]

> But his wife looked back from behind him, and she became a pillar of salt.
> **Genesis 19:26**
> [KJV]

Chapter 17 instructs Lot and his family in escape, that they should move to the mountain, not looking back, lest they become 'consumed'. In chapter 26, Lot's wife disobeys, and looks back, consequently being consumed into a pillar of salt. Not much is spoken about Lot's wife in scripture. The only other reference we have to her is from Jesus, in Luke, where we are instructed to "remember Lot's Wife". We don't know her name, age, or even much about her family background, but to me, this makes her story even more important, as every single character in The Bible has several levels of wisdom to impart - what do the few lines that are written about her mean? What does Lot's wife teach, and how do we harvest the "fruit" from her story? One of the important messages I believe, is a warning against empathy.

The Bible doesn't specify why Lot's wife looked back; however, my contextual understanding of this text would lead me to believe that Lot's wife had empathy for the people in Sodom; the place she and her family had called home for the past (24+?) years. Although the people of Sodom were wicked, from the text you can see that Lot and his family were not estranged to them. When the men of the city surrounded his house, enquiring of the angels, they addressed Lot directly. With a bit of cultural knowledge of the time, we understand that women were traditionally in charge of the social calendar, and as such, would be the ones who knew the names of neighbors and their children, birthdays etc. Whereas men of the time could have very 'surface' relationships with the community at large, it was the women who really kept things running, socially. So to Lot's wife, I can imagine that these weren't just people – these were people with names, faces, stories and shared experiences – these were 'friends'.

I would further hypothesize that Lot's wife didn't *necessarily* look back using her neck, but with her heart. I would suggest that

Lot's wife's calamity was that she allowed her heart to open up; and as it went out to the people of Sodom and Gomorrah, in empathy, she inherited their affliction as a result. The image to the left depicts the people of Pompeii, who were 'turned into salt' when the volcano erupted – these are not statues, but actual people, who are preserved because of the volcanic brimstone ash clouds – remember, empathy allows you to step into someone else's shoes and experience their issue. This is <u>not</u> a positive thing. Lot's wife was commanded to follow her husband to the mountains – she was given a word which should have caused her to become elevated; instead whilst walking in the valley/ the low place, she allowed herself to feel empathy - considering an inane thought in her heart, it was manifested into her life. As a man thinketh in his heart, so is he.

As a new covenant child, Lot's wife also speaks to me about faith, (or the lack thereof) and how forgetting or purposely taking your attention off the word of God, even temporarily, can mess up your destiny. We have to keep our eyes fixed on the place that God has said He is bringing us to – for some of us this may be a prophetic word, a dream or a vision – it is so important to meditate/ focus on this, until we see His Word accomplished in our lives. You start meditating on the past, and guess where you end up?

This is no different to what we find ourselves doing all the time. We make excuses for loved ones, friends, family members, and those who find themselves in a familiar situation. In our 'respect' for the difficulty of their situation, we disrespect God, and His ability to have ultimate compassion on every single individual on this planet – in this sense we commit blasphemy, as this is akin to denying Jesus, the individual, personal savior provisioned for all. Empathy means that because we 'feel' a person's situation, we are moved, (by empathy, at said situation) usually resulting in lowered expectations; both that individual, and God. We come into agreement with the harshness of that situation, confessing how 'difficult' it is for someone in their position; negating God's boundless love, compassion, and therefore hope. In doing so, we have turned into a stagnant Christian – a pillar of salt, unable to be poured out, or affect change, we conform ourselves to mediocrity: having a form of Godliness, but denying the power [2 Timothy 3:5]. It is time for us to cast 'self' to the ground, literally breaking the alabaster box, so that our fragrance can be released and never again return to the lifeless monuments which people look upon, as a representative of a seemingly 'dead' Kingdom – one with which they have no desire to affiliate.

…Remember Lot's wife.

WARFARE

This may seem like a strange place for the sub heading of 'Warfare' to appear. However as stated earlier in this chapter, empathy really can undermine the power of God in an individual's life, and this is especially evident when it comes to warfare. Believe it or not, we can empathize with the enemy and his *power*, over and above our reverence of God, and it is very likely that this is something you, like I have done on a daily basis for many years. If in your previous teachings regarding warfare, you started with the different kingdoms of demons, or the power structure and skillset of a throne vs a principality, or how demons operate in the water kingdom, vs demons in the air kingdom, you have been educated from an empathic, and therefore flawed stance. You have missed the most important revelation. The first lessons of warfare are found in The Word of God, and they all have to do with YOU. Whenever God mobilizes an attack through his people in The Bible, the emphasis is <u>never</u> upon the other side, but like with Moses, God is more concerned with showing you 'what is in your hand'. There are countless other examples from Gideon to Elisha, expounding this same theme. Through the power of God, you are justified and equipped to tread on snakes and scorpions [Luke 10:19], confident that no weapon fashioned or formed against you shall prosper [Isaiah 54:17], and with no fear for the arrow by day, nor the terror by night, nor the pestilence which walketh in darkness [Psalm 95:1-10], because we are seated as joint heirs, with Christ [Romans 8:16–17], sacrosanct in the fact that neither angels, nor principalities nor powers or any other creation can keep us from this love [Romans 8:38-39], we stand as representatives of The Kingdom of God; as superconductors - enforcers of His will on earth.

Now I know some esteemed demonologists and deliverance ministers will disagree with me, mostly based upon experience; what they have seen and encountered – demons of different strength, intellect, stature and ferocity. Respectfully, whilst honoring their

77

experience, I would echo the earlier sentiment, that whilst the world attests that experience is the best teacher, The Bible put this onus on The Holy Spirit. "Who is this that darkeneth counsel by words without knowledge!" [Job 38:2] For a self-professed demon-slayer – even with a proven track record, to super impose their own experience based doctrine upon God's teachings, is folly. Although The Bible tells us that we should not be ignorant of the devices of the enemy, nowhere does God instruct an individual or a nation to meticulously study their enemy. To what gain? We already know who the victor is – why not instead become wise in the strength of God. Not only is this an insult, or a second-guessing of God's sovereign power and His love toward you, but It is very dangerous to 'consider', or allow yourself to be wowed by the enemy's structure of power. This very quickly sows seeds of fear and caution through the spirit of empathy into the heart of the observer. There are things, which as Christians, we need to learn how to filter and tune out. Some of us are more versed in the nature of the enemy, than they are in the nature of God. This is a sad shame.

You need to stand, sober, resolute, and unwavering in complete faith, understanding and conviction in the word of God, and what He says, in complete love, concerning you, and your life – this is the only, Biblical way to engage in warfare. The Bible says:

> Put on the whole armor of God, that you may be able
> to **stand** against the wiles of the devil.
> **Ephesians 6:11**
> [KJV]

> Therefore take up the whole armour of God, that you may
> be able to **withstand** in the evil day, and having done all,
> to **stand**. **Stand** therefore, having girded your waist with
> truth, having put on the breastplate of righteousness
> **Ephesians 6:13-14**
> [KJV]

Traditionally we think of armor as the protective uniform of a soldier or warrior who fights in battle. According to the scripture, the <u>primary purpose</u> of the full armor of God is not protection from external attack, but a protection from our own internal infirmities; a garment which proactively assists in helping us to **stand** in Jesus, <u>wherein lies true protection</u>. The reality is, Jesus has already secured us through faith, in victory. ALL we need to do is stand, resolute, believing, and with faith, and see what God has already done, unfurl. Warfare is not an argument or a negotiation, but an enforcement of truth. It is the active recognition of an agreement between you and God – in reality it has little to nothing to do with the devil. Our reason for engaging in warfare should always be the love of God, His will and His word – Satan should never be the impetus! We are only enforcers of truth – God's truth. You can only do this by standing in, as and for the truth, which is Jesus. That is the only TRUE law of spiritual warfare. Yes there are lords, princes and kings in the demonic world, some 20 feet tall, some unimaginably intellectually astute; however, as a representative of the King of Kings and the Lord of Lords, even the lowliest in The Kingdom of God outranks the most exalted in The Kingdom of darkness [Genesis 3:15, Romans 8:16–17] et al.

Standing in Jesus; the full armor of God, as children of the New Covenant, we are provided with weapons [2 Corinthians 10:4-6]. Now a weapon is an external piece of apparatus, which can be used to inflict harm to the point of fatality – most often used as a means to bring a hostile party to surrender and as a means of protection. A gun, a knife, a cannon: weapons are external entities which we can use in combat. The above scripture says that the weapons we are provided with in warfare, are not carnal (of this world), and there are several scriptures where we see some of these 'weapons' in action – Elisha and the legion of non-carnal horses and chariots of fire [2 Kings 6:17]; Daniel's visitation, [Daniel 10:13] and in Revelations, where we see angels used to subdue and defeat the dragon and his *angels* [Revelation 12:7-9]. This is why prayerful life is so important when it comes to warfare – not that prayer is in and of itself a weapon. Remember, a weapon is an external entity, but prayer is the request for and the subsequent downloading of divine tactics and strategy, which will be used in warfare, by your weapons. Prayer is akin to the bullets in a gun, or that which sharpens a sword, ready for battle – if you do not live a prayerful life, your weapons will be practically obsolete; after all, we know from scripture that the word of God feeds angels [Psalm 78:25, John 6:35, John 6:48-51]. By praying from a God-defined pure heart, we pray the word of God – we pray Jesus, which 'feeds' our weapons.

Consider that given these weapons are provided by God Himself, in love, that these weapons are prefect, and more than adequate to secure victory. Unlike modern carnal warfare, in the realm of the spirit we are the only ones with the weapon of mass destruction, serving a Kingdom with an impressive <u>one hundred percent</u> success rate in combat; so when we **stand** in authority, the enemy quakes.

The truth is, Jesus did not engage in warfare; enforcing sozo to show His power. Yes, His power was evidenced, but scriptures tell us the reason Jesus healed, delivered and ultimately saved, was because He was moved by compassion – possibly the greatest gift ever given to the heart of a Christian.

CHAPTER 7

COMPASSION

So Jesus had compassion on them, and touched their eyes: and
immediately their eyes received sight, and they followed him.
Matthew 20:34
[KJV]

Compassion is often confused with empathy. This is akin to the
comparison drawn between the phenomena of God's favor and the
world's standard of *luck*. Empathy is a non-equivalent equivalent for
compassion; in that they are both tools, used by individuals in an
attempt to understand and alleviate the suffering of others. However,
their origins, functionality, and their end, expose their difference.
Compassion is always the only *appropriate* tool for the job.

Compassion is the ability to tap into the heart of God
concerning a situation, resulting in movement, in the power
of God's love, to restore divine order in said situation.

Unlike empathy, where you can only do "your best", to help
a person in a difficult situation, when an individual is moved by
compassion, miracles happen, the impossible is resolved and the
Glory of God descends. The old adage says there are two sides to
every story - probably more aptly put, there are always opinions,
stances, sides... and then there is the truth. Empathy empathizes

81

with opinions, stances and sides. An individual who has been psychologically abused within a relationship in the past, will blinkeredly empathize and 'side' with someone who appears to describe or embody a similar situation, blinded to the whole truth of the multiple dynamics concerning said situation. Because you are literally tapping into the heart of God, compassion ALWAYS operates out of truth, justice and peace. The love of God is incapable of taking sides! [Acts 10:34, Romans 2:11, Deuteronomy 10:17, Job 34:19]

Because you tap into, and operate from the heart of God, as opposed to that of another individual, there is no risk involved in the act or lifestyle of compassion – none whatsoever. No contamination, no corruption, and no risk of infection. In compassion, you are free to act as a conduit of, and partake in God's love with no fear. In this place of compassion, you will be able to minister to the disenfranchised, the homeless, and the demonically possessed, in the fullness of God's love; seated as a joint heir with Christ, there is no fear of failure, or retaliation from hostile parties.

CAPERNAUM

When Jesus was rejected by Nazareth [Matthew 4:12-16], He and His family packed up and moved to Capernaum; a fishing village in Galilee, northern Israel. This became His new home, and the base of His ministry. It was here that Jesus encountered the Centurion, great of faith [Matthew 8], and the paralytic man who had been lowered through the roof of the house where He was teaching [Mark 2]. Capernaum is a place that will often come up, when the topic of compassion is discussed; and it is easy to see why. Although the people of the village were a heathen and hard hearted people, Jesus was so moved by compassion in Capernaum that it is speculated by most theologians that Jesus did more miraculous works in Capernaum than the sum total of miraculous works done elsewhere. Either way, we know it was the most noted of the top 3 *'cities wherein most of His mighty works were done'* [Matthew 11:20-24]. Capernaum [caper'-na-um (Gk. from Heb.)] can be literally translated into *village of Nahum*; Nahum meaning 'Comforter'. The Hebrew understanding of Capernaum is: village of consolation; shelter of comfort; covering of compassion; covering of repentance. In the Hebrew paradigm, these words have the same root. It is interesting, because through Nahum (comforter), we get compassion – we know from scripture that The Comforter is the Holy Spirit [John 14:26]. In the dwelling place of Nahum, [where The Holy Spirit dwells], compassion abounds. This is why the enemy wars for the heart of believers. If we cannot show love or compassion one to another, we 'frustrate' The Power of God, not only in our lives, but also in the lives and hearts of the unbelievers in our sphere of influence [John 13:35]. It is no surprise therefore that the act or lifestyle of compassion is, in fact, what one observes when an individual operates out of the nine simultaneous personalities/ attributes of The Fruit of the Spirit. We should also make note of the fact that Capernaum was a fishing village - remember the great commission, and that in Matthew 4:19, Jesus says, *Follow me, and I will make you fishers of men*. When one operates in compassion, fishing is made easy. A brief study on the area, will reveal that Capernaum was at the center of Jesus' ministry in Galilee; whose name means 'circle', 'region' or 'parameter'. Compassion was at the center of the encompassed ministry of Jesus – it is a very important precept to understand.

It is not enough to just speak Jesus, or to confess Him out of our necks, but it is with the inward assimilation of Him that we begin to manifest compassion, whereby we can demonstrate the Love of God in truth, and in power as a 24/7, deliberate lifestyle. If there is something which we learn from Capernaum; the covering of compassion, we should remember that Jesus made it His dwelling place. Every time we operate in compassion, we are exposed to, and expose Jesus to the world.

As mentioned previously, in compassion, we operate from the heart of God; <u>not</u>, as with empathy, from our own heart, and so we operate out of faith – a system of absolute knowing, based upon God's word, as opposed to our partial knowledge, based upon our own experience. The Bible says we know in part, and we prophesy in part [1 Cor 13:9], but God knows all. He knows how to facilitate healing to the heart and mind, the body and the soul of any given individual on the face of this planet, at any given time - and because our heart is open to God, in compassion, that timeless, boundless, infinite truth is exactly what is being related, and manifested though us, into that individual's life.

	Empathy	Compassion
Mechanism	Individual's heart opens to the other person's (OP)'s <u>situation</u>	Individual's heart is open to God, and operates though His open heart toward the <u>OP</u>
Result	Stimulation. The OP may 'feel' better. Possible positive outcome from experience based insight.	The Kingdom of God made manifest. The door is opened for OP to experience the revelation of healing [*sozo*], in all areas of their lives.
Contraindications	Limited action, with risk of contamination, which can cause <u>*dead* problems to be resurrected,</u> or fresh inhabitations because of the unguarded heart.	**None.**

Have you ever seen a badly behaved child out in public, often being ignored by a defeated parent who has clearly negated the tenacity needed to be able to train that child into obedience? What we are observing is indiscipline – that of the parent, which has become manifest in the child. This is no surprise, after all, the Bible tells us that deep calleth unto deep, [Psalm 42:7] and that iron sharpens iron [Proverbs 27:17]. There are three understandings or compartments to the human makeup – the soul, the spirit and the body. Consider that when 'Pastor x' is ministering, as the congregation listens, deep is calling to deep, and iron is sharpening iron – Pastor X's soul is ministering to their souls, his spirit to their spirits, and his flesh to their flesh. If Pastor X has indiscipline manifested in his soul, although his mouth is ministering one thing, his soul is ministering another. This is firstly *understood* by the souls of those who are being ministered to, and secondly *received* by the souls wherein indiscipline is already found – those predisposed to/ susceptible to indiscipline. Just like the unruly child in the earlier example, there is no way for the pastor to control the indiscipline he has allowed to be trained into his soul, in a public place, having never taken the time to erect discipline in private. The same is true with indiscipline of the spirit, and indiscipline of the flesh – why do you think Pastors who contend with sexual desire are never short of sexual partners in the churches they visit? As the pastor preaches, though the word is being ministered through his disciplined spirit, the sexual appetite of his indisciplined flesh is calling to and sharpening against the sexual desire (where present) of the indisciplined flesh in the congregation. Without even a conversation, it is a guarantee that this pastor will have his fleshly desires met.

As Christians, this is very poignant. In our daily interactions with the other people, what are we *really* ministering? And that's before we take into account that according to Dr. Albert Mehrabian, author of *Silent Messages*, 93% of communication is non-verbal. This means that even with your mouth closed, all three aspects of your person are still communicating – a sobering thought.

Are people who come into contact with you, being ministered
The Kingdom of God, or being yoked into bondage?

If we are to operate in the realm of compassion, it has to be all or nothing. There is no point having compassion in our soul, but not in our flesh – in this we present an unjust balance, which is an abomination unto God. For us to truly burn with compassion it requires us to accept Jesus into every fiber, joint and sinew, so that compassion isn't just a momentary feeling, but a lifestyle which permeates every waking, and even sleeping moment.

This is the shortest chapter in the book, but that is because compassion really is that simple. IF you submit to God, wholly, it will only be a short while before compassion overtakes you and becomes very much a part of your daily life. The key to acquiring this compassionate heart, truly is submission.

Let us endeavor to make compassion a lifestyle choice.

CHAPTER 8

WORSHIP

I'll bring you more than a song// for a song in itself is not
what you have required... I'm coming back to the heart of
worship// it's all about you// it's all about you; Jesus.
Matt Redman – The Heart of worship
Copyright © 1997 Thankyou Music.

In addressing THC one area we cannot avoid is that of worship. For
many, this chapter will be the least palatable, and hardest to read,
as the misconceptions surrounding this "ethereal principal" are so
heavily and dogmatically programmed into the hearts and minds
of most believers, according to their house, that the understanding
has been lost. Today in our churches, worship has de-volved, been
marginalized, and mutated into a miscegenation of dance, music and
monetary giving. For the sake of clarity, I'm not saying music, dance
and monetary giving are not worship - they absolutely are *expressions*
of worship; however, to say that "music, dance and monetary giving
is worship" is not a holistic statement. Everything we do is worship.
<u>EVERYTHING</u>. Worship is a language which emanates from
the heart of man, and therefore whether you are standing as an
abstinent single person, fasting for three days, or even the simple
act of brushing your teeth, you are engaging in worship. This is
why idolatry is so easy - because we are naturally given to worship:
it's what we do. In the same way that breathing or heartbeat is an

involuntary bodily function, worship is an involuntary function of our inner man. We can CHOOSE to give our worship to God, and as individuals who call ourselves 'Sons', or 'Daughters', this is the challenge - total submission.

There is a posturing of the heart, where it becomes so tender toward God that truly, every breath, every waking moment; every heartbeat is a worship <u>to God</u>. This is true submission, when even your bladder and bowel movements are in and of themselves a worship. For many of you, that may seem a step too far; however, do not let THC deceive you. Do you not think God realizes that he made us with a bowel and a bladder? Do you not know that YOU are His best, His final work? God rejoices over us, and loves us - all of us, furiously. There is not one part of us that God is coy of - He loves us *completely*. Everything we do, bar none, has the *potential* to be a worship unto God. This understanding is one of the keys that will enable us to be more cognizant of who we are, and truly throw off the shackles of THC and worship God in spirit, <u>and in truth.</u>

In worship, there is a tenderness of heart toward God; a lightness and a sweetness that reverberates or feeds back into the soul, the spirit and the body – we feel good, almost ecstatic during worship. Some experience this during praise and worship at church - but truly, as believers our heart should never leave this state. When our hearts take a posture of worship, the Glory of God, and with it, Heaven, is really able to manifest through our hearts, into our souls and our physical man.

> Then I said, I will not make mention of him, nor speak any more in his name. But his word was in mine heart as a burning fire shut up in my bones, and I was weary with forbearing, and I could not stay.
> **Jeremiah 20:9**
> [KJV]

> And they said one to another, did not our heart burn within us, while he talked with us by the way, and while he opened to us the scriptures?
> **Luke 24:32**
> [KJV]

This is what it feels like to be a true worshiper – The Word of God is in you, and you are constantly burning with excitement and enthusiasm toward sharing God's love with others. The more you try to quench it, the more it intensifies. This is not just a *feeling* for 'praise and worship'. As adults, many will know what it is to have burned with anger, remorse, or indeed lust, when a specific individual or incidence comes to mind. Yet very few of us can attest to that same burn of worship when we wake up, grateful to God for another day or when we get out of bed with breath in our lungs. This is not something we can put on, but rather something we foster in our hearts, over time. It is a wonderful thing to cultivate the habit of being grateful; not from the angle of unworthiness, but as a receptive child of privilege – it will really help your worship.

Remember how Moses' face glowed after coming into the presence of God [Exodus 34:29-30]? The same glory which was exposed to Moses, is the same glory which manifests in our hearts, when its posture is conducive. This same glow (we're talking about a literal glow, radiance, luminance) can therefore manifest in our hearts, our souls, and even our physical bodies. Jesus told us:

> Blessed are the pure in heart: for they shall see God.
> **Matthew 5:8**
> [KJV]

Remember, whatever you have planted and hidden in your heart, is what will eventually end up manifesting into your life. Consider Enoch. The Bible says give, and it shall be given unto you.... pressed down, shaken together and running over [Luke 6:38]. If you kept your heart pure, as a vessel of worship to the true and living God, postured only toward Him, your harvest; good measure, pressed down, shaken together, running over is <u>God</u>.

As you begin to engage your heart more, the understanding of the heart waxes great, and the five non-physical senses of the heart are activated – smell, taste, sight, hearing and sense/feel. However, your heart has to be discipled by the Holy Spirit in order for you to properly understand what your heart's five senses perceive; otherwise you do not contextually interpret what is being conveyed. In this state, we can misinterpret what we see, smell, taste, hear and feel. An example of this would be a child who *sees* fire, *hears* it crackling, *smells* burning, and *feels* its warmth, but can't contextually process what this means. The next step would be for the child to try and grab the fire, and attempt to put it in his mouth (*taste*). This will of course lead to calamity, pain, and unnecessary suffering. This is exactly what happens to people that use reality altering drugs, and no different to what happens to every single one of us, in the THC state. Now, the cantankerous and argumentative brother/ sister at church is getting dreams, visions, laying hands and or prophesying – accurately, BUT their understanding is not subject to God. Be aware.

In seeking a deeper revelation and a closer walk with God, we should be mindful to respect the process, and not get ahead of ourselves. It is a great thing to 'open one's eyes' – wisdom is a phenomenal gift to get, BUT in all thy getting; get understanding [Proverbs 4:7]. Real, tangible worship as previously described takes dedication, over time – it is a daily conditioning process. We should not become like *the wicked and adulterous generation, who seek after a sign* [Matthew 16:4], but our love for God, an attitude of gratefulness, our desire to please Him and to see His will made manifest on earth, should spearhead our devotion to a lifestyle of worship.

> The sacrifices of God are a broken spirit: a broken and a contrite heart, O God, thou wilt not despise.
> **Proverbs 15:30**
> [KJV]

LET US WORSHIP

In The Bible, the word most frequently used, denoting worship, is the Hebrew word *"Avodah"*. The word literally means to work, or to be in service of. The word paints a picture to our understanding that worship is not an "act", but a continuous manifestation in everything that we do. Words derived from the same root, will give us an understanding into what worship truly is: An *oved* is a worker. *Evid* is a slave. *Avdut* is slavery. *Avodat Elohim* is the service or worship of the true God. *Avodah zara* is literally strange worship including idolatry and corrupt or feigned worship. *Avodat Elillim* is idolatry, the worship of false gods. *Avdut* is bondage, slavery to Satan. The key theme found in scripture when describing worship, is work.

According to physics, <u>work is a measure of force exerted to another person, place or thing</u>. We may labor with our hands, our feet, our physical bodies, but work as it relates to *Avodah* is the force in what we do, which we choose to give unto God (or not). Everything we do requires some form of force – even our thoughts, and so you can see there *can* be worship, to God, in everything. Whatever you do for work, whether you are an administrative assistant, a plumber or a hairdresser, please understand that these are all opportunities to worship. It is the posturing of the heart which defines to whom that worship is addressed. Even the acts that we traditionally think of as worship, such as the ministration of song, or even philanthropy and missions are only directed to God, via the heart. The Bible tells us to give "as our heart purposes" [2 Cor.9:7], and so the person who goes on twenty missions sows thousands of dollars to the cause, yet in the heart there is strife - as wonderful as his/her works are, that was <u>not</u> worship, directed to the true and living God.

> And though I bestow all my goods to feed the poor, and though I give my body to be burned, and have not charity, it profiteth me nothing.
> **1 Corinthians13:3**
> [KJV]

STRANGE FIRE

And Nadab and Abihu, the sons of Aaron, took either of them his censer, and put fire
therein, and put incense thereon, and offered strange fire before The Lord, which he
commanded them not.
Leviticus 10:1
[KJV]

My heart was hot within me, while I was musing the
fire burned: then spake I with my tongue.
Psalm 39:3
[KJV]

When this heading was put into my spirit, I didn't necessarily know what to write. Yes it is profound, and it instantly conjures images of a strange type of ungodly worship, but it was too vague for me to write about. God then began to speak to me about the architecture of the OT Tabernacle and the Temple, and bought me to the Golden Altar of Incense, which was not only a shadow of Christ [Eph.5:2]; [Gen.8:21]; [Heb.1:3], but also the believer's heart. Pure gold is a *precious* metal. It has very little (electrical) resistance: it is a *superconductor*, meaning that it transcribes (electrical) information from point **a)** to point **b)** with little to no deviation from how it was represented at the source. It is *sonorous*, meaning it has the ability to produce a sound of a rich, loud and deep, to a high sharp and piercing quality. Gold is highly reflective of both heat and light, and its *reflectivity* makes it an expert at representing a truth, accurately; and it is a relatively soft, *malleable* and *ductile* metal – it yields, and is able to be pulled, even to the point of wires, without breaking. Pure gold speaks of something which has been through the process of refinement, and its very existence is a testimony. It is also the metal which represents The Most Holy Place and The Holy of Holies – the place where the commandments, and indeed the presence of God were found. The properties of gold perfectly describe the yielded heart of man. This Holy Place comparison, again reinforces the sentiment of Psalm 119:11, where David says that he has hidden the word in his heart – The Most Holy Place of man.

Proverbs 20:27 says that the spirit of man, is the candle of The Lord. A candle can be used to illuminate but also, to ignite. The spirit ignites the heart, and it is our job not only to keep that fire burning, but also to keep our heart guarded, so that the fire remains pure. This guarding includes making sure that our spirit is kept holy, so that the ignition doesn't actually contaminate the heart, and once the fire is lit, making sure that the integrity of the flame is not compromised by external influence. The heart is the golden altar of fire upon which our incense is percolated up to Heaven. The strangely postured heart – a heart under the influence of THC, elucidates a strange fire before God, and therefore, the incense which is laid upon it, 'makes no sense' – its meaning and beauty is lost. The fire is profaned, and therefore, so is the incense (worship). If you continue reading in Leviticus 10, you will see that God killed Nadab and Abihu, not because of the incense, but because of the **strange fire**, which was in and of itself an offence, and therefore defiled the incense which was being offered. Even the most costly incense is defiled by a strange fire - it is extremely important to keep one's heart, with diligence, and with understanding. Knowing that everything we do is worship, we can see how the inappropriately postured heart will taint our worship; even our living, so that it is an unceasing, daily offence before God. Our living, unbeknownst to us, can cause a foul smell in the realm of the spirit, for no other reason than the posture of our hearts.

There is a very literal sense to scriptures like 1 Corinthians 6:19-20, which speaks about our bodies being the temple of God.

Bless The Lord, o my soul, and forget not His benefits. -Psalm 103:2

The Holy Spirit dwells in the temple [Rom. 8:11], and He regenerates [John 3:3-5], He anoints [1 John 2:27], He baptizes [Acts 2:17-41], He empowers [Micah 3:8], He sanctifies [Rom. 15:16],

He comforts [John 14:16-26], He gives joy [Rom. 14:17], He gives discernment [1 Cor. 2:10-16], He bears fruit [Gal. 5:22-23], and He gives gifts [1 Cor. 12:3-11]. We are called as a royal priesthood [1 Peter 2:9], and it is our job to *keep* our temple in a way which is most conducive to hosting the Holy Spirit.

In 1 Corinthians 10:23, Paul says. "All things are lawful for me, but all things are not expedient: all things are lawful for me, but all things edify not." There are issues, paradigms and ultimately idols, which people, even Christian people battle with. The reality is that with the fulfillment of the law, all things *are* lawful; however in maturity, we need to ask: is it expedient? Does it edify? No man is condemned for the law, but as referenced in Matthew 7:21-23, condemnation is the fruit of the choices we make, which are not expedient for, and edifying to relationship with Christ - we do not sin against the law, but against Jesus, the word – our new covenant.

We can spend our days doing anything of our personal choosing, but one day our substance will be tested and those of us who proclaim love for God, will be required to show forth evidence. In the same way that a husband who does not adapt, mold and become 'one flesh' with his wife, but instead prioritizes his desires, pursuits and lusts, has shown greater love for his self than for his wife, many Christians miss the revelation, and do this exact thing with God. Knowing that the standard is holiness – wholeness with and in God, [1 Peter 1:16, Leviticus 20:7] what steps have you made in its pursuit? In this understanding, there is no depth of addiction which cannot be reasoned away by faith, hope and in love – because the greatest of these is love. There is no height of illicit behavior, which cannot be insisted against, in the power and authority of God, by choosing love over lust – obedience is better than sacrifice, which is obedience to the word of God, as opposed to sacrifice because of the law.

THE PSALTERY AND HARP

I can't tell you the number of times I've heard musicians disproportionately berated because they use their gift for music, in the secular realm. And by secular realm, I'm not talking about propagating non-Biblical principles, such as fornication, greed and violence, but individuals who do not deviate from their integrity as Christians, yet do not perform 'Christian music'. These are individuals, who are in the world but not of it – their music is wholesome, their image is family safe, but because they operate in the secular arena, people take issue. Now please hear me out on this one – I know for many of you this is an open and shut case: musicians should only use their gift for gospel music; but do you then hold up others who use their gift in the secular realm to the same standard? What of the grounded Christian individual who has a gifting for mathematics, and becomes the senior financial officer at a (secular) multinational blue chip company, or the gifted (Christian) scientist who becomes a (secular) doctor, or the baptized, born again individual, blessed with the gifts of persuasive argument and articulation, who goes on to become one of the nation's greatest (secular) barristers? The truth is, the people mentioned in the last three examples would more than likely be celebrated and praised for their achievements, whilst the musician in the same scenario would be berated and scorned. Why is it that we hold this "double mind" when it comes to what is a right and seemly use of one's gift? And more importantly, <u>does The Bible hold the same double mind?</u> Because of our marginalization and misinterpretation of worship, we have confined the gift of music for use within the gospel arena only. Worship is a posturing of the heart; *not* just words, or a melody. Just because someone says Jesus, doesn't mean that at that moment Jesus was being worshiped, and just because someone does not mention The Lord's name in a song, does not mean that that it was not a Glory to Him. We cannot use our five physical senses to rationale or make arguments for and against things of the spirit.

The issue at hand is that <u>All</u> Christians should take Jesus with them. God says that He has exalted His word above His name, and so although we place so much importance upon lip service, God is more concerned with us being a representation of Jesus, His word. It is a great shame to be afforded a platform, and not take the love of God with you, manifested through compassion in all that you do, and to be a proud representative of His Kingdom as your gift takes you before great men and the multitudes - BUT many secular Christian artists do, and have seen fans, managers and record executives converted, because of their influence. Just because we do not see a ministry, does not mean it is not powerfully active, for Christ. Remember this - It is no greater a shame for a secular musician to not represent Jesus, than it is for you or I: have you shared the gospel with your co-workers? Do your colleagues know Jesus? What about your family? God is no respecter of persons, and so expects <u>all men</u> to be good stewards over what he has proportioned to them. A Christian who refuses to represent Jesus is a shame, universally, irrespective of profession. A friend recently told me about a well-known secular artist. He doesn't sing Gospel music, yet his music and his image are wholesome. He does not practice or promote perverse acts like fornication, and is in fact happily married, and has been for some time. His music has given him a platform, and his gift has truly brought him before great men. He holds concerts which pack out arenas, and at the end of those concerts, he holds an altar call, and a team of pastors come out and pray with those who have chosen to give their lives to Jesus. Someone may look at this example and say, 'well he is a minority', but truthfully, how do we know? I've known of this artist for <u>years</u>, and I never knew that he did altar calls at the end of his concerts. I had no idea that his ministry was alive and kicking, for Jesus. I have been to 'gospel concerts', where less actual reverence for God was shown than this! We open our mouths, and we judge other's salvation, but we cannot see the integrity of their hearts, and we have *no idea* how God is using them to minister His gospel to individuals, and even the masses. The reality is that there are some places that Gospel music will not reach, and some hearts that it will not minister to. The word says:

> Behold, I am sending you out like sheep in the midst of wolves; be wary and wise as serpents, and be innocent (harmless, guileless, and without falsity) as doves.
> **Matthew 10:16**
> [AMP]

We are called to be salt and light to the world [Mat.5:13-16] – there are cracks and crevices of society who need to be ministered to with wisdom, yet without compromise. For some people, the name of Jesus is a trigger, at which they will switch off. We need wisdom to be able to minister to these people in a way that will change their hearts to a place where they will confess the name of Jesus, of their own volition.

The fact is, we honor God every time we use our gift, in integrity and to His Glory. Excellence in this pattern, is therefore in itself, a worship to God.

I've heard the argument that Lucifer was the "praise and worship leader" in Heaven, before he was kicked out, and therefore we need to be wary with the gift of music, lest the musician becomes like Lucifer, and forgets that he is a servant of; and NOT God. Now firstly, addressing the issue of arrogance and the spirit of self-servitude - this is a human condition, and an issue of the heart. Insisting that an arrogant pianist plays in the praise and worship team, as opposed to playing backup for a secular musician is only a change of employment - now you just have an arrogant pianist playing worship music. The sweetness of the music he plays is a glory to his self, NOT God. Again, I say, don't let THC blind you to differentiating between skillset and anointing. People can live abhorrent lives before God, yet still (in this example) play the piano with effortless mastery, which would have you on your face, in tears during praise and worship. The Bible tells us that "Gifts and callings come without repentance" [Romans 11:29], and so unfortunately, the vehemence of a gift is not a marker of whether or not that gift is subject to the spirit of God. This means that tongues, the accuracy of a prophecy, the poignant arrangements of the musician or songwriter, or singer are NOT a confirmation of God's anointing on an individual's gift, or life. Every time this individual plays from his uncircumcised heart, he elucidates a 'strange fire'. This worship is profaned, and taints the congregational worship act with noxious black soot as it ascends into the heavenly realm, as opposed to the 'fragrant smoke' associated with prayer and with worship.

The Bible doesn't actually say that Lucifer was the *minister* of music in Heaven. However, there are several scriptures that let us know that Lucifer had a propensity and possibly aptitude toward music [Ezekiel 28:13, Isaiah 14:11-12, Isaiah 14:12 & Job 38:7]. Ezekiel describes him as an 'anointed cherub' and as having 'walked back and forth in the midst of fiery stones.' These 'fiery stones' are seen in Ezekiel 1:13 and Isaiah 6:6. According to Ezekiel, Cherubim essentially look like a cloven-footed humanoid, winged bull, or eagle, or lion, depending on which of the four faces you saw [Ezekiel 1:5-11]. Here we can see where the myth of Pan, the Greek and Roman god, who was always depicted as either a goat or bull-like humanoid creature playing music, possibly came from. If we are using this example of Lucifer (who from scripture we know had an association with music) to dissuade musicians from playing in the secular arena, then by the same merit, we should also dissuade Christians from being politicians or any type of non-church leadership figure, because it is clear to see from scripture, that Lucifer - the principality who convinced *one third* of the angels in Heaven to revolt, was a charismatic leader and politician. This would be a ridiculous stance to take, yet it is one taken regularly when it comes to question of the appropriation of the gift of music.

Music is described by some, as being *emotional*, and can therefore influence us beyond the realms of our minds, and so there are groups of individuals who have an irrational fear of ALL non-gospel music. When we talk about something being emotional, or interacting with our emotions, we are talking about our soul. The key phrase here is therefore *resonance*. The word resonance literally speaks of the ability to provoke or evoke a response, in this case as it pertains to imagery, memories, or a physiological or emotional response. We should therefore recognize that <u>everything</u> perceived by the five senses has the capacity to be emotional. It could be a smell that reminds you of a loved one, or a taste that 'takes you home'. A texture that makes you feel weird; colors which make you feel warm; and yes, a sound which elucidates a certain feeling. There are examples of resonance independent of a pre-existing association, (Morphic Resonance) and resonance because of one (Sympathetic Resonance). An example for me, is mohair – for those of you who don't know, mohair is a type of material that was used a lot in the 80's in knitwear. The feel of mohair is emotional to me, because it takes me back to being a child, and falling asleep on my mother's lap, my head on her mohair cardigan. This is because of a pre-existing association – Sympathetic Resonance. There are certain smells, like freshly baked bread, or a warm buttery cinnamon sugared pastry, that *even* if you have never smelled them before and there is no pre-existing association, will generally elucidate the same emotional response, when smelled. This is the phenomena of Morphic Resonance. All five senses have the capacity to be emotional – not just hearing, and therefore music. If we are prone to being easily led by our emotions, then that is the issue – ineffectual modulation of the heart. As Christians, we cannot blame external influences for our behavior; for we have not been given a spirit of fear, but one of love, and of power, and of **a sound mind** [2 Timothy 1:7]. <u>When we demystify the misconceptions surrounding these 'golden calves' that we have erected in our minds, we can enter into true worship, free of fear.</u>

CHAPTER 9

THE UNTOUCHABLES

And the LORD sent a plague upon the people because they
made the calf which Aaron fashioned for them.
Exodus 32:35
[AMP]

Why do you call Me, Lord, Lord, and do not [practice] what I tell you?.
Luke 6:46
[AMP]

Pulling down the high altars, killing the golden calves, and
extinguishing the desire that caused them to ever find residence
within us is the intention of this chapter; by exposing the idolatrous
systems which plague the hearts and mind of man. It's something
that we have all been guilty of at some point – even subconsciously:
to *try* to preserve areas of our lives from the will of God (total *sozo*);
attempting to hide our nakedness, like Adam in Eden. The issues we
refuse to deal with, which sit like gold-gilded ornaments (gods) in the
display cabinet of our heart – protected and preserved: unchallenged.
Areas which we choose to sweep under the carpet and ignore; literally
turning a blind eye to the devil in our own house. The problem is
that withholding anything from God, which manifests itself as a
lifestyle of contention – from lying, to suspiciousness, anger, bad
attitude, hurt and addiction – even fear, may seem trivial, but is in

fact one of the most dangerous and deleterious forms of idolatry we can ever <u>allow ourselves</u> to become practitioners of. The <u>all sufficient</u> liberty afforded by Jesus, as a covenant of God's Love, through Calvary IS the ultimate reality, and so in living a lifestyle where we continually and consistently manifest untruths concerning this reality, is evidence NOT of God and His sozo, but of an idolatrous system, which seeds and bears fruit after its own kind.

The fact that these illegitimate systems have infiltrated The Kingdom, is evidenced in recognizing that we have allowed the five-fold ministry, as ordained by God, to mutate into a board of temple prostitutes; turning tricks in order to appease these *gods*, and keep the system ticking over by offering these services in exchange for monetary recompense. Every Sunday, the objective is clear: make the people feel good so they will continue to patronize the house.

The reality is, when we come into the House of God we should be able to fellowship, be challenged and encouraged in our faith, and engage heaven in intercourse; encountering God in a tangible way. But most will settle for *metaphorically* mirroring Onan [Genesis 38:9] – indulging in sensationalism that feels good in the moment, but leaves you empty, weak, and impotent: unable to produce in the week ahead. This is however, just a macrocosm – a blown up manifestation of the state of the heart of man; *The Latter House* of God.

Please read this chapter with a heart poised to receive truth.

IDOLATRY

I went to India some years ago. I was on the board for an organization that plants churches, takes care of orphans and runs an orphanage in India. So I went there to teach and to visit, and as I went through the villages, out into the rural areas, I saw these shrines on the side of the road, built to regional false gods over certain jurisdictions and in those little shrines were chicken feathers and blood and they would sacrifice animals in there and they would leave food and money for the little god of that neighbourhood. There were idols everywhere. People were down at the beach, covered in paint, worshiping, literally, the ocean as the tide went in and out. I mean, there were festivals everywhere. People had idols in their homes. It was unbelievably clear to me that this was a culture so steeped in Hinduism that it was just filled with idolatry and I thought to myself, "How could anyone live in this culture so constantly surrounded by idolatry?"

And I was talking to one of the pastors' wives and they were both Hindu converts. She's a very articulate, intelligent, very great woman and I said, "Well have you ever been to the United States?" She said, "Yes, but I don't like to go, so I don't go very often." I said, "Well, why do you not like to go to the United States of America?" She says, "I can't stomach the idolatry..."
Excerpt from 'Resisting Idols, like Jesus', a Sermon by Pastor Mark Driscoll

The first time I heard this sermon by Pastor Driscoll, it sent shivers up and down my spine. My eyes had truly been opened. Traditionally, idolatry is something we attribute to other people and cultures – it is easy to look to the Orient, with their reverence of the Buddha, or to Africa and its fetish statues, or indeed India, and its pantheon of over 330 million gods; idolatry and/or paganism is something that poorer, less educated people do. No rational 21st century *western* person would ever get involved with it. If only that statement were true. Idolatry is, generally speaking, a needs based system, in that as a need arises, an individual who has not FULLY put their trust in God, will seek out a 'god', which will meet the need, offering them 'salvation' from the fear of not having that need met.

We give 'the flesh' a lot of stick, but idolatry is usually born out of the soul, which wants to understand; who will love me; who will feed me; who will provide raiment and shelter? The soul is concerned with the wellbeing of the whole person – this is a good thing, but has no direction, no vision and no foresight, without the ministration of the spirit, via the Judgment of the heart. In THC, because the spirit of God, vicariously through the spirit of man, is not able to effectively minister through the heart; the soul involves the individual in idolatry. This could be a simple act, like the individual who idolizes their car, because of how the car makes them feel (that they are perceived by other people). The car (idol) gives them status, and in return, they give that car their worship. Remember, worship is a posturing of the heart, and so there is a difference in someone looking after their car, and in the posturing of their heart, doing so as thanks unto God, as a good steward over what He has provisioned; and the person who idolizes a created thing. Pastor Driscoll coined the adage, that 'idolatry is usually the pursuit of something which is otherwise good', and this is true. Idolatry is *voluntary* bondage to a thing, because of the perceived benefits, including its ability to save from a perceived 'hell'. Like the person who refuses to deal with their obvious anger issue, because of the perceived benefits (power, authority, security…), and the fear that they would become a 'doormat' if they released their issue over to God. <u>In whose name do we truly trust?</u>

An illustration given of this same phenomena, is an individual who finds themselves in *depressed hell,* and in the pursuit of deliverance, they turn to the idol of 'Comfort Food'. The idol appears to do the job, but after a while the individual ends up in *fat hell,* which in turn delivers them back into *depressed hell.* They turn to a new idol – 'The Diet god', which promises to deliver them, and sure enough, within months the individual is no longer in *fat* or *depressed hell.* It is not long before the new issue of *hungry hell* manifests, delivering the individual back into *depressed hell,* and the cycle continues. This is the systemic, cyclic nature of idolatry, which has individuals building their own pantheons of idols in a very short space of time. Ultimately, idolatry never works, and so you will be forever 'making-good' for your gods. We place so much importance upon obtaining good things, which God says He already has for us, but in our impatience, we become idolaters. This is exactly what Paul was talking about in 1 Corinthians 10.

(PROBLEM)
"I need to feel validated and appreciated as a man"

⇩

(god OF SOLUTION)
Family/ Ministry: Become a father.

⇩

(SECONDARY PROBLEM)

"My wife isn't giving me the respect and attention that I require."

"My congregation don't validate me in the way I need them to"

⇩

⇩

(☺ SECONDARY god)
Infidelity

(☺ SECONDARY god)
Soulish preaching/ emotionalism

In idolatry, the individual's heart is postured to receive a savior – a lot of us do this with money for example. This is why The Bible curses the *love of money*. Money isn't the issue, but our desire for it relative to its ability, as a benevolent and kind god, to endow us with happiness, things, and long life.

There is an erroneous belief system in The Kingdom, in which people assert that a person's gift is proof of salvation, and so we find it strange when a gifted prophet, apostle, teacher, pastor, or evangelist is caught doing something nefarious. People knowingly encourage individuals into marriage, or ministry for example, turning a blind eye to the fact that there is an underlying issue; under the delusion that this office will rectify the issue, with time. This in itself is an example of an *idolatrous mindset*. There is NO name under which a man can be saved, no title, no office, bar the name of Jesus. An example of this is the cultural belief that people marrying young, 'saves' the individual from fornicating (often a misunderstanding of 1 Cor 7:9

is used to support this doctrine). Now, there is nothing wrong with two mature and committed young individuals getting married – it is definitely a Biblically sound idea to get married young which we can find echoed in scriptures such as Proverbs 5:18 and Psalm 127:4, but if someone has an issue controlling their sexual urges, marriage cannot deliver them! Idols will help you to disguise a problem, or temporarily transfer it, but only God can truly deliver - salvation makes you free! If you use marriage as an idol to free you from the hell of promiscuity, then you are put in a bondage to that person; becoming dependent on 'marriage' to keep you disciplined. Statistics suggest that 1 in 10 married men cheat on their spouses when they are pregnant. Why? Because those 10% likely had an unresolved issue with sexual restraint before they entered into marriage, and so when their wife was unable to fully satisfy them sexually (for a period of time), they found out that marriage did not solve their issue - they were never delivered. Similar statistics can be found during miscarriages and times of bereavement. THIS is not the image of *sozo*, but the fruit of idol worship.

What are your idols?

REASONABLE EXCUSES – THE GOLDEN CRUTCH

"And lest I should be exalted above measure through the abundance of the revelations, there was given to me a thorn in the flesh, the messenger of Satan to buffet me, lest I should be exalted above measure. For this thing I besought the Lord thrice, that it might depart from me. And he said unto me, My grace is sufficient for thee: for my strength is made perfect in weakness. Most gladly therefore will I rather glory in my infirmities, that the power of Christ may rest upon me. Therefore I take pleasure in infirmities, in reproaches, in necessities, in persecutions, in distresses for Christ's sake: for when I am weak, then am I strong."
2 Cor. 12:7-10
[KJV]

A golden crutch is something which people hold onto, that serves as a *reasonable excuse* for why they or someone else is not currently, won't or can't manifest the fullness of what God has promised to and for them; or perform their reasonable, dutiful service to God. The Bible says that we can do all things through Christ which strengthens us [Phill 4:13]. Yet those with a golden crutch will append the verse with an asterix (*) in order to make room for it. The crutch is essentially a replacement for Christ, and so whereas we can do all things, leaning on His strength, those with a crutch will lean onto its 'strength' as an excuse for why they cannot.

There are two categories of golden crutch: **perceived**, which is something such as sex, race/ cultural background, age, height, and **actual**, such as sickness, poverty, appetite (eg: physical, sexual, addictive personality), and education. This is a major issue, because faced with God's word, those with a Golden crutch will judge in favor of the golden crutch in their hearts, thus usurping the power of God, for that of the golden crutch.

I remember having a conversation with a good friend of mine about a famous secular entertainer who at the time was in and out of court due to allegations made surrounding his relationship with the numerous children which kept his company. Mid conversation, my friend interjected with a very interesting statement:

"Whilst none of us know if he is guilty or not, IF he is, it isn't really his fault, because he was abused too as a child."

Almost 10 years later, that statement still ruminates in my mind. This is a perfect example of 1) a golden crutch, and 2) how we generally view them as a 'get out of jail free card', a license to be outside of the perfect will of God. Whilst very few people on the planet actually KNOW what went on with those children, IF the alleged events did take place, then the entertainer in question was fully accountable for what he had done, regardless of whether he was abused as a child or not. Please do not mistake my candor for a lack of compassion – abuse is a terrible thing for anyone to have to endure, especially a child. However this 'golden crutch' does not exempt anyone from God's standard - there are no sick notes in The Kingdom of God.

Just like with a broken leg, a crutch is only supposed to be with you for a season, until you are able to stand in healing, at which point it is handed over to the physician. If you never let go of the crutch, you will never be fully healed, and you create an unnatural dependency on something you no longer need, based upon something which has long passed away. In THC, instead of being handed to the physician, the crutch – even the perception of a crutch is made golden – ornamental, sacred... precious. So many times, I have heard Christians - even Christian leaders talk about a situation, and close with 'Well, he/she/I'm only human!', when The Word of God tells us that he who is in Christ is a <u>new being/ creature</u> [2 Corinthians 5:17] - yes, even the perception of *being human* is a golden crutch for many.

Paul's 'Thorn in the flesh' [2 Cor. 12:7-10] has become the pericope of numerous illegitimate doctrines and opinions of 'mediocre sozo' in Christendom today. Wherever there is a 'Golden Crutch', there will likely be someone brandishing this scripture as a warrant to explain away their shortcoming. This means that all manner of sexual perversion is justified because of abuse; sickness is fine, in spite of the fact that we have already been healed 'by His stripes', and mean heartedness is justified because of past hurt. The misrepresentation of this scripture has really caused a lot of unnecessary suffering within The Kingdom, whereby even leaders have justified people living a tormented life with one leg in and one leg out of *sozo*. This is not the will of God; an unjust balance, and therefore an abomination before Him.

<u>What was Paul's thorn in the flesh?</u>

Many highly esteemed theologians have espoused that Paul's thorn in the flesh was a God-given sickness which He refused to heal him from, and infer that this is the 'infirmity' referred to in 2 Cor. 12. However, this is a gross misinterpretation of the text - a misrepresentation which would put this verse at odds with the rest of the NT, including the declaration of Isaiah 53:5 and 1 Peter

2:24 – we have already been healed, because of Jesus' stripes. This sets a dangerous precedent – now, when even after prayer my situation still doesn't meet up to God's promise and expectation for my life, I am justified in concluding that the lack of sozo shown forth in my life, is God's divine will, REGARDLESS of what The Word says. From obesity to unforgiveness (even when you know the other party is 100% to blame), fornication to homosexuality – all of which can be 'spun' into a thorn which God has desired to be made manifest in your life, to His glory. According to 2 Corinthians 12:7, Paul tells us the thorn in the flesh was a 'messenger of Satan', in the Greek, *angelos*, a physical entity, either angelic or human, which is why Paul says in verse 8, that he prayed three times for (him) to depart. The thorn was NOT a sickness.

There are several other instances in scripture where this exact terminology, thorn in the flesh, is used, referencing **people** [Num. 33:55; Josh. 23:13; Judg. 2:3]. The colloquialism of thorn in the flesh would be pain in the neck, or pain in the behind – a figurative pain as opposed to an actual pain. It is also important to note that although God told Paul that His grace was sufficient to deal with the thorn, the text does not say the thorn was given by God.

The verse then continues, '*gladly therefore will I rather glory in my infirmities, that the power of Christ may rest upon me. Therefore I take pleasure in infirmities, in reproaches, in necessities, in persecutions, in distresses for Christ's sake: for when I am weak, then am I strong*". This seems to support the sickness theory. However looking at the Greek, the word used for infirmity can indeed mean sickness [1 Timothy 5:23], but it is also translated as *lack* or *inadequacy*. An example of this can be found in Romans 8:26; "The Spirit also helpeth our infirmities." In this case the infirmities are to do with us not knowing what to pray for – the infirmity of a 'finite' mind, and so the Holy Spirit will bridge the gap of our inadequacy. Paul says he will 'glory in his infirmities', because God is glorified through them, and lo and behold, in 2 Cor. 11, Paul actually lists these infirmities, which include imprisonment, stripes, shipwrecks, stoning's, and the subsequent (temporary) weakness and pain. None of the listed things are sickness, and even with persecution, as David reminds us in Psalm 34:19, "The righteous person may have many troubles, **BUT** The LORD delivers him from them <u>all</u>."

Paul's 'thorn in the flesh' was not a golden crutch. Though Paul reasoned that the thorn was given lest he be 'exalted above measure', 1 Peter 5:6 says, "Humble yourselves therefore under the mighty hand of God, that he may <u>exalt you in due time</u>." God not removing this 'messenger' from Paul's life, would have in fact been the impetus which caused Paul's ministry to thrive even more, as the level of persecution doled out by this individual would go on to cause Paul to insist more upon God, wherein his ministry would look less like Paul, and more like the God he was preaching to the people. In the same way that God instructed Elijah to drench the sacrifice in water (in the midst of a 3 ½ year drought!) before He sent fire from heaven, or in the same way that He cut down Gideon's army to 300 men before they went forward to conquer an army of over 135,000 Midianites – for in our infirmity, His strength is made perfect.

The problem with this type of idolatry is that it is a mindset, which means that we *can* even turn God-given gifts into golden crutches – this is exactly what many do with grace and with mercy, a notarized 'sin license' to the corrupted hearts and minds of those under the influence of THC. A golden crutch will excuse us from duty because of a perceived infirmity, but it is the will of God that our perception and subsequently our reality, changes to the point of absolute resolution in the fact that we truly have NO infirmities in Him. They who *wait upon* [**serve** – as in **wait**er] The Lord will renew their strength; they shall mount up with wings as eagles; they shall run, and not be weary; and they shall walk, and not faint [Isaiah 40:31].

Lord, remove every notion in my heart, which exalts itself above the infallible promise and reality of Your Kingdom. Help me to cast off ALL infirmity, and find true strength in You.

NOW MAKE [FOR] US A KING (CELEBRITISM IN THE KINGDOM)

> **3** For the time will come when they will not endure sound doctrine; but after their own lusts shall they heap to themselves teachers, having itching ears; **4** And they shall turn away their ears from the truth, and shall be turned unto fables.
> **2 Timothy 4:3-4**
> [KJV]

The title comes from 1 Samuel 8, where the elders met, and decided that God should give Israel a king, *like the other nations*. This displeased God – YES, it was God's plan for Israel to one day have a (human) king [Deut. 17:14-20; 28:36, Ezekiel 37:24-25] but trying to produce fruit out of season; this act was no different to Sarah handing her hand maiden over to Abraham. It wasn't yet time for Israel to have a (human) king (God Himself had stood as Israel's King, whilst David was becoming 'ripe'). However, because of the grumblings of the people, God granted them a King of their choice - Saul. This is exactly what happened with the Golden Calf of Exodus, and no different to what happens today. We set our affections on the systems of this world, desiring to incorporate, or have our version of what we have perceived to be 'good' from the secular world. Ironically it was Saul, who *ignored* the word of God which emphatically commanded him to wipe out the Amalekites: *'utterly destroy all that they have, and spare them not; but slay both man and woman, infant and suckling, ox and sheep, camel and ass'*, and instead decided to save what <u>he perceived</u> was good and of use to The Kingdom [1 Samuel 15]. For this same reason, there are value systems, various doctrine and structures of hierarchy with <u>no</u> <u>Biblical basis</u>, which have worked their way into The Kingdom.

Today, in Christendom, we have made our leadership, our musicians; anyone who shows an ounce of refulgence, into our 21st century golden calves. We open our hearts to them, without question, and there is no discernment of their fruit. We have all done it - found

ourselves in a conversation, where we have said something, which when challenged; after frantically searching through the nearest Bible, we realize is not actually a Biblically founded paradigm in our heart and mind, but something which we heard our favorite Pastor say once. The issue is that at the moment we receive a word, the onus is upon us to substantiate that word with the purported originator. If someone tells you something new about an individual you love, naturally, you would check with the individual in question that this information is correct. If you didn't, then there would be legitimate grounds for an outside observer to question the integrity of your relationship. Truly if we love God, and someone exposes something new to us about God's word, then there should be a strong desire within us, to confirm these words, as would be needed to erect God-ordered faith. If we have cleaved onto an ideology, just because our favorite Pastor has made utterance only, then we have put our faith in man, which The Bible says is folly [Psalm 118:8, 146:3-5]. God says He has exalted His Word above His Name, yet we vainly call upon His Name without establishing our petition upon His Word. No man comes to The Father, except through The Son (The Word of God) - this is why many of us, with a foreign, alien word, *even* with faith, cannot enter in. We are to test every spirit - is this word meat for me? If we have been guilty of trusting in man, and therefore establishing out faith in a man; we need to check our hearts.

We worship these idols we fashion under the guise of honor and respect. The reality is, we stand so many times in a month for the man of God, First(?) Lady, visiting pastors, elders etc. in our churches, and we do it faithfully, but spiritually most of us faint when it comes to standing for God, His promises and His precepts.

The Bible says, put on the full armor of God, so that you may <u>stand</u> against evil [Eph. 6:10-17] - this is what true warfare looks like. Those who cannot stand are going to find it extremely difficult to walk the path of righteousness *without slipping*. How come we can give a sacrificial offering of $200, but we can't sacrifice the rottenness of our hearts, to God? Why is it so rare to find an individual who would *wholeheartedly* (not just an emotional response) get up and leave their past behind during a meaty word on a Sunday, yet those who would put their hand into their back pocket, run up, and slap a $50 bill on the altar are numerous? The Bible says where a man's treasure is; his heart is there also [Matt 6:21, Luke 12:34]. What we perceive as being valuable, we give to our golden calves, but our real treasure, the thing which Heaven and hell war for; our heart, our soul, spirit and body, we withhold.

> *"Today I would like to challenge you to dig deep, and sow the biggest offering of your life. To those who feel led, sow your heart, in its entirety, back to God."*

There are numerous examples of leaders who have temporarily fallen from grace because of something they have been alleged to have done, or failed to do. Whenever this happens there are always individuals who *blindly* run to defend their leader's innocence, with no information, knowledge or revelation concerning the alleged event(s). The reality is we can swear by no man; only God. In the same measure, no one can take the side of offence and say that the leader in question definitely did do 'x', because again, no one knows, save that person, any involved parties and God (unless The Spirit of God has revealed it), what actually went on. Yes, we stand for our leaders, but not because they are infallible and incapable of doing any ungodly thing - that is unbiblical. Even a righteous man abides in his free will, and is able to decide in his heart to do something deliberately unrighteous, at any time. We stand for the integrity we have perceived him/her to have in the past, the God that we discern in his/her life and honor them for, and we pray to a God who hears, cares, and brings revelation: to establish His order in the situation at hand, and for His love to take control. Anything more, or less is a sign of someone irrationally protecting his/her personal golden calf. This is also true of the person who insists that an individual is guilty, when they have absolutely no solid proof or insight to back up their postulations – in this case their golden calf may be anger, stemming from a hurt in the past that the individual refuses to let go of, which now causes them to irrationally tar everyone with the same brush; without considering the matter in a purified, yielded heart.

With age, comes the understanding of price, but only in maturity do we begin to understand and appropriate value. Put differently, as we become older, we know how to count, and so we can *quantify:* "my dad is bigger than yours!" We speak highly of ministers because of their membership, their book and DVD sales, and the grandeur of their place of worship. Like David in 1 Chronicles 21:1-4, or the woman in Ezekiel 23:20, we are stuck in the paradigm of quantity as a stand-alone system, whereby worth is attributed. Saul could see the numerousness of the spoils from the Amalekites' land: healthy sheep and strong cattle, but he failed to grasp their true value contrasted against the word of God, instructing him to destroy them. No matter how vast the pen of livestock Saul had acquired, this was all negative equity; and so less than worthless. In maturity, we learn value, meaning we can now *qualify* - I see your 30,000 members, but where is their fruit? Where is salvation? Where is discipleship? We see beyond the tangible, and we discern worth, where one shall chase 1,000 and two, 10,000. Saul should have recognized that although the sheep were healthy, strong and great in number; neither one, nor the sum were suitable for sacrifice to a Holy God. It is here, in maturity, (which is itself the pursuit of maturity) where we cease from supporting defunct, illegitimate systems, such as the *strange priesthood* we see manifest today; wherein for example, preachers don't spend time seeking a word from God, but instead, <u>preach definitions</u> under the guise of being 'deep'. Baselessly dipping in and out of *the Greek* and *the Hebrew*, weaving a confused tapestry; a garment for a confused people - a garment which will not withstand the harsh cold of winter, provide shelter in rain, nor substantially cover against the power of the air… [Selah]

It is in maturity that we destroy our idols, snuff out our strange fires, and (re)turn our affections to God.

THE ISSUE OF BLOOD

> But we are all as an unclean thing, and all our righteousnesses are as filthy rags; and we all do fade as a leaf; and our iniquities, like the wind, have taken us away.
> **Isaiah 64:6**
> [KJV]

The above scripture speaks of the good works that we often use to vindicate ourselves, or another person, as being good. "I know my Pastor hears from God – just look at what he does for the community", when good works are not, by any Biblical standard, standalone proof of anything. For the sake of clarity, God definitely does expect us to do good works, and celebrates us for it – even the preceding verse [Isaiah 64:5] says that God meets he who *joyfully* works righteousness. The issue here again, is the heart. The Bible tells us that we should not be wary in our well doing [Galatians 6:9], after all, it is our reasonable service; nothing extra, and therefore truly there is no boast to be made. When we try to present our good works to God, it is then that they become an offence [Romans 3:27; Ezekiel 33:13; Titus 3:5]. 'Filthy rags', doesn't really give the full understanding of how much of an offence this is, but if we examine the Hebrew text, the word filthy comes from the word *iddah*, which literally translates as 'the bodily fluids from a woman's menstrual cycle'. The rags are '*beged*', meaning rag, or garment. In trying to make boast of our righteous acts, what we are doing is akin to presenting God with a bloody feminine hygiene product, or a garment soiled with menstrual fluid. This would not just have been an unpleasant and slightly bizarre thing to do; offensive in and of itself, but when you look at this contextually, at the time the text was written, menstruation was seen as an unclean thing. This would be akin to a burnt sacrifice of a pig, an unclean animal under the old covenant, in the temple.

Nid(d)ah, is a Hebrew word for a woman in the process of menstruation. A Nidah was seen as unclean, and there are several laws laid out in Leviticus as to her conduct, for seven days during her time of menstruation (for as long as the menstruation lasts) [Leviticus 18:19, 15:19-30, 20:18]. These included the Nidah's food being prepared and all of her housekeeping duties suspended and delegated to a third party, because a Nidah was unclean, and therefore everything she touched became unclean; culminating in a special purification ritual at the end of the seven days. There was an understanding of cross contamination, and so there was a cleansing process for everything that the Nidah came into contact with, lest it contaminated another individual for seven days, who could in turn contaminate another, and so on. We know that these laws are all shadows, and so we understand, as children of the New Covenant, that although these laws have been fulfilled, there is still wisdom we can learn by studying the Old Testament. Rules relating to women are interesting because we can usually garner some revelation about conduct within the body, the bride of Christ.

This is really a message for leadership, and is probably more poignant now, than ever. We have seen so many instances of Apostles, Prophets, Evangelists, Pastors and Teachers, who have experienced some form of trauma in their lives: a divorce, an allegation, skeletons coming to light etc., yet they continue in ministry, in spite of their inner turmoil. There are times when our leaders are wounded, bleeding as they stand on the altar, and no one thinks this strange – in fact, they are congratulated for their courage and bravery in the face of adversity. However, there is an issue of blood, which makes them Nidah. In this instance, someone else should be delegated to prepare meals for the house, lest the Nidah and her family become malnourished whilst she is sat down; relieved from all housekeeping duties. Leviticus says that anyone who has intercourse with a Nidah, becomes unclean. Intercourse simply means to encounter/ an interaction – when more than one 'course' intersect. Conversation is an example of intercourse. This is where we get the term 'sexual intercourse', which has now been shortened to just intercourse in the modern vernacular. What we see is a very clear image; that when we open up our inner man to receive from a person who is in the process of bleeding, we open ourselves to contamination.

I gave an example earlier in the first chapter, of a pastor who spoke about how she would interact with her husband if she ever remarried; *her money* in a separate bank account, no cooking, no cleaning etc. This is an individual manifesting the signs of Nidah. Another way of expressing cross contamination is to *indirectly empower*. This pastor, her heart and mind still not fully healed into the reality of The Kingdom of God, *indirectly empowered* others, in her bleeding state, to get married; yet circumvent The Word, their partners needs, the unique needs of the relationship, and to withhold whatever they deemed (in their broken state) necessary. Those individuals will then go on and *indirectly empower* (contaminate) others, and so on. This is how false doctrine spreads like a thick impenetrable fungus in The Kingdom. The reality is, the compromised meal should never have been served up in the first instance – this Pastor should have been relieved of her housekeeping duties, sat down and fed, until her issue disappeared. Both the leadership and the congregation were at fault in this scenario.

This is a symptom of a **system** which does things as rhetoric, and has forgotten the **reason**; the initial impetus which made them come together to worship in the first place. It is truly time for us to remember love, and in remembering the why/ *the motive*; the how/ *the method* will always be correctly established.

BABYLON

The heart is deceitful above all things, and
desperately wicked: who can know it?
Jeremiah 17:9
[KJV]

Wherefore the Lord said, Forasmuch as this people draw near me with
their mouth, and with their lips do honor me, but have removed their heart
far from me, and their fear toward me is taught by the precept of men.
Isaiah 29:13
[KJV]

This people draweth nigh unto me with their mouth, and
honoureth me with their lips; but their heart is far from me.
Matthew 15:8
[KJV]

For I do not understand my own actions [I am baffled, bewildered].
I do not practice or accomplish what I wish, but I do the very
thing that I loathe [[a]which my moral instinct condemns].
Romans 7:15
[AMP]

There is a mysterious system of worship, which readily infests the
heart in THC. It is silent and deadly in its operation; like a serpent,
it lays dormant, waiting, watching for an opportune moment to
strike. It is *insidious*, and is a master mystic, almost invisible to even
the trained eye. The system is called Babylon, the mystery of iniquity
and, unfortunately, Babylon is a physical reality in the hearts of
many Christians today. Webster's defines mystery as:

mys·tery
noun \\'mis-t(ə-)rē\

- a religious truth that one can know only by revelation and
  cannot fully understand
- a secret religious rite believed (as in Eleusinian and Mithraic
  cults) to impart enduring bliss to the initiate (2) **:** a cult
  devoted to such rites

- something not understood or beyond understanding :ENIGMA
- *obsolete* : a private secret
- the secret or specialized practices or ritual peculiar to an occupation or a body of people <the *mysteries* of the tailor's craft>
- a piece of fiction dealing usually with the solution of a mysterious crime
- profound, inexplicable, or secretive quality or character<the *mystery* of her smile>

The word 'mystery' also speaks of a veiling, and truly, Babylon will enshroud evil under its cape and cast its blanket before the light in the heart of its victim. Babylon is like the dance of Salome to the heart – mysterious, captivating and alluring, to the point where an individual is seduced into covenant. The Bible doesn't actually mention how Salome danced - the seven veils as seen in Hollywood interpretations of the story are non-Biblical, but it is easy to see why this "myth" stuck.

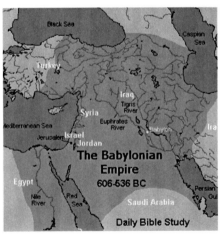

The Kingdom of Ancient Babylonia was referred to as 'the cradle of the human race', and when we actually look back at its geography, we can see that' it was strategically structured to encapsulate the Garden of Eden [Gen 2:8-14]. Understand that it has always been the plan of the enemy; through Babylon, to inherit the place where you walk and converse with God. Yesterday is was the Garden of Eden. Today, it is the heart of man.

Babylon is a very ancient kingdom, representing the seat of an old principality. Although we see many *great* kingdoms that have come after, <u>Babylon is the parent spirit</u>. As referenced in King Nebuchadnezzar's dream [Daniel 2], Babylon is the 'Golden head' – we all know that the head controls the body. Therefore, understand that when Babylon is established in a heart, it can deploy Persia with its sexual perversions and spiritual mysticism, Greece and its spirits of intellectual cantankerousness and empty mythology, and Rome with its military strong men, and tactical warfare. These inhabitations affect the mind, the will and the emotions of the host in a horrific way. This is what would be classically termed, 'occupation'.

Occupation: *control and possession of hostile territory that enables an invading nation to establish military government against an enemy or martial law against rebels or insurrectionists in its own territory.*

Understand that the spirit of Babylon, as manifested in all of its Kingdoms, is a principality, and so deals with the ability to conquer and subdue. The same spirit, and the desire to dominate will be present in the host. We have heard a lot about the spirit of Jezebel, but what many people have not considered, is that Jezebel is a representative of a kingdom; a queen, and an emissary of the (spiritual) kingdom of Babylon, and so <u>in deliverance, we are not just looking to remove Jezebel, but the kingdom which sent her</u>. The fact that Jezebel has manifested means that she was deployed from a kingdom – a queen sits on a throne, and in the case of Jezebel it is a throne of Babylonian origins. It is nothing for the vile witch who required John the Baptist's head, to require a heart as her throne room.

The kingdoms of Babylon, Persia, Greece and Rome, all traditionally practiced castration; a technique of sterilization, which cuts off the 'seed' of an individual so that maximum loyalty to the throne is assured. Babylon will terminate and abort every good plan in the heart of an individual, replacing that which is destiny and purpose with a 'phantom'. Whereas living out one's purpose and destiny in God will enrich secure and 'complete' the life of an individual, the aim of this phantom is only to pillage, plunder and ultimately destroy. Castration comes so that for all your work, you would have amassed and achieved nothing of your own. To help you grasp what is being said, consider the cuckoo bird, who does not build her own nests, but much like a parasite, waits for a different species of bird to leave her

nest unguarded. The cuckoo will remove some of the eggs from the nest, and replace them with one of her own. The bird will return to the nest, and unwittingly keep the eggs warm until they hatch. When the cuckoo chick hatches, it will instinctively remove any eggs or hatched chicks from the nest by pushing them out – in fact, the

A greedy Cuckoo baby (L) is fed by its unwitting surrogate Reed Warbler mother (R).

cuckoo hatches with a 'hollow back'; an aptly designed 'scoop' for this task. The result is that the bird will pour all of its time and energy into raising the one cuckoo chick. These chicks grow at an alarming rate, have insatiable appetites, and will actually grow up to five times the size of its 'surrogate parent', but the 'parent' will continue to work tirelessly to feed its chick, to the point of exhaustion - and often times, death. Many destinies have been hijacked in the same way by the spirit of Babylon, via the use of spiritual castration; the sprit of Babylon laying the egg that will hatch into Persia, Rome or Greece, which, even in its infancy will work to first terminate the destiny of the host, and eventually the host herself. *We take authority and come against every spirit of castration and 'the phantom' in the name of Jesus, AMEN.*

The kingdoms work as one unit; synergistically. Persia, for example, known for its love of spice, perfume, vibrant color, sensuality and rich, indulgent tastes, will know how to flavor sin, make it visually appealing and palatable to the heart and mind of its host. Greece will educate the mind in the art of self-hypnosis and impart the *gift* to intellectualize sin. Rome with its military mindset to conquer, will build an iron fort for these ideologies – a strong man, in the heart and mind of the host, and working together with Greece and Persia, plot out the strategy of a successful takeover, cementing Babylon in victory.

If you take a look at Babylon: its strategies, its mysticisms, its intellectualism, its militia, its technologies, its perversions, its wealth and fine tastes, through the keen eyes of an analytical thinker, you will see that Babylon The Great; the Mystery of Iniquity, was not formed to make you sin. Sin can be erased by Calvary, and a repentive heart. All that work was toward the expected end of getting you to sin, past the point of no return. There is one sin which The Bible says God refused to make provision for; where Calvary will not save you: the sin of apostasy (two if you count blasphemy of The Holy Spirit [Matthew 12:31] to be different to apostasy).

The Bible says of apostasy:

> ⁴ For it is impossible for those who were once enlightened, and have tasted of the heavenly gift, and were made partakers of the Holy Ghost,
> ⁵ And have tasted the good word of God, and the powers of the world to come,
> ⁶ If they shall fall away, to renew them again unto repentance; seeing they crucify to themselves the Son of God afresh, and put him to an open shame.
> **Hebrews 6:4-6**
> [KJV]

In order for you to commit apostasy, you need to have pressed into a deep revelation of God – not everyone is actually able to commit apostasy, because they have not yet walked in the fullness

of God that apostasy requires. This is why Babylon sits, as a patient serpent in the hearts of believers, for sometimes twenty or thirty years, before the opportunity is right for it to strike.

If we look back at Daniel 2, and Nebuchadnezzar's dream, we know that this prophesied the progression and eventual fall of Babylon, but as 21st century Christians, there is clear message for us in this text. In the diagram to the left, you will see a representation of the statue that Nebuchadnezzar saw in his dream. The head of gold, the breast and arms of silver, the stomach and thighs of brass, legs of iron, and the feet of mixed iron and clay. In Revelation 18, the fall of Babylon is foretold. Although this statue represents five different kingdoms, we are in fact looking at a WHOLE MAN. In the same way that we, the body are a manifestation of The Head - Christ, the statue represents the fullness and totality of the golden head; Babylon. When looking at this statue, what God showed me is a schematic diagram of apostasy – what Babylon Stands for. The man represents the vehicle, out of the presence of God, symbolized by the Old Testament temple and tabernacle. From the head downwards, we see:

Golden Head

- The inner sanctuary, or most holy place, represented by Gold; this is where the Ark of the Covenant and the Golden bowl of manna are found. The fullness of The Glory and Majesty of God is here; where the presence of God is so thick it can kill an unrighteous man. You must leave this place, in order to apostatize.

Silver Chest and Arms

- This is a step backwards, into the nave, or holy place, where the priests could be found making sacrifices. Silver is the metal associated with the tribe of Levi, who were set aside for the priesthood, to make offerings on behalf of the people. 1 Chronicles 29:4, for example, speaks of the silver overlaid walls in the priestly quarters. Silver has always represented 'atonement', and the process of purification. Psalm 12:6 says, "The words of the LORD are pure words: as silver tried in a furnace of earth, purified seven times", in which we also see Jesus, The word, purified seven times. We have to walk away from atonement before we can apostatize.

At this point, we acknowledge that just as your flesh will prevent you from entering into the holy place; conversely, leaving the most holy, and then the holy place, signifies that one's **flesh** has fallen away; born out of The Kingdom of God, delivered **head first** into The Kingdom of darkness (pictured left).

Brass Stomach and Thighs

- Brass represents the outer court; the brazen laver [Exodus 30:17-21], the brazen altar [2 Chron. 4:1], the ten bronze wheeled stands [1Kings 7:27, 2 Chron. 4:6], the 'bronze sea' and the twelve bronze oxen which carried it [1 Kings 7:23, 2 Chron. 4:2-5], and the hollow bronze pillars 'Boaz' and 'Jachin' [1 Kings 7:21, 2 Chron. 3:17]. Both brass and bronze are impure metals, and Biblically are symbolic of judgment, and sin, eg: [Deut. 28:22-23]. Although brass and bronze are two different alloys of copper, the Hebrew word *Nachosheth*, makes no differentiation between them. The Bible says that Moses held up a brass/ bronze serpent on a stick, which cured the people of the scorpion poison which came upon them, as a result of their *sin* [Num. 21:9]. John 3:14-15 compares this to Jesus on the cross, who took on our sin, and was nailed to a tree. This is a place of reflection and contemplation, where your sin is stripped bare, and held up for you to see. We need to leave the outer courts, negating the process of introspection and cleansing, in order to apostatize.

Bronze also represents *the gate to the temple, which is called beautiful* [Acts 3:2]: we are leaving the temple grounds. At this point, we recognize it is an individual's **soul** which has fallen away; born out of The Kingdom of God, delivered into The Kingdom of darkness.

As symbolized by the imagery of the Babylonian statue (above left), at this point, an individual been 'delivered' into The Kingdom of darkness, waist high - yet without legs. This sentiment is echoed in Acts 3: the lame man (without the use of his legs) outside the beautiful (**bronze**) gate. This is also where the apostles declared, '**silver** (holy place) and **gold** (most holy place) I have none.."

Iron Legs

- Iron represents the gates into New Jerusalem, which 'opened by themselves', and Peter walked through in Acts 12:10. This is a representation of Jesus, and the fact that through him, The Kingdom of God has swung open its gates for us. The fact that we are now dealing with iron is again indicative of the fact that we have now left the temple; 1 Kings 6:7 lets us know that iron was not used in the building of the temple, and it cannot be found within the listings of decoration. Interestingly, 1 Chronicles 22:3 tells us that David prepared iron in abundance for nails for the doors and gates and joining in the temple. Iron Nails, again, talk of Christ, Calvary, and being reconciled to God. In order to apostatize we need to deny Christ, The Kingdom of God, and the eternal promise of Calvary.

To walk away away from Calvary is to fall away, in one's **spirit**: the first house, to which salvation [sozo] came. Born out of The Kingdom of God, into The Kingdom of darkness. At this point, we no longer call ourselves sons and daughters – we have become a bastard child; <u>however</u>, at this point, through grace, we can still repent and become born again.

Feet of Iron and Clay
- Iron and clay are the iron bars of bondage, and the miry clay of hopelessness. Iron and clay represent our past, and the fact that God rescued us from it. Psalm 107:16 is just one example which speaks of the iron bars which imprison, and in Psalm 40, David gives thanks to God for taking him out from the horrible pit, and the miry clay; placing his feet upon a rock.

In order to apostatize we have to, as a bastard child, in ungratefulness, walk away from the purest instance we knew of love, literally spitting in the face of God. At this point, the backslidden individual has not only taken on and embodied the full image of Babylon, but also the likeness.

I was then taken to Genesis 9:23:

> And Shem and Japheth took a garment, and laid it upon both their shoulders, and went backward, and covered the nakedness of their father; and their faces were backward, and they saw not their father's nakedness.

God was showing me the posture, of shame and regret; versus the posture that one takes, in confidence, as they commit apostasy. He began to speak to me about orientation, and the fact that in the schematic diagram of Nebuchadnezzar's dream, you are actually walking backwards, head up, eyes open; watching the statue being erected, from the head down, and wilfully choose not to abort the process. You stand in the holy of holies, which was built as a very small and narrow place, which the high priest squeezed himself into once a year. In the most holy place, you walk into a heaviness of the presence of God, where your nature <u>will</u> change, and you begin to reflect the likeness of God which James 1:17 describes, where there is literally *'no shadow of turning'* – you cannot physically turn in this part of the temple. To exit the most holy place, you have to walk backwards. In apostasy, you do this eyes open, (revelation/ fully aware) backwards, through the holy place; through the outer courts past Boaz and Jachin; out of the beautiful gates; out of the saving grace of Christ and the promise of The Kingdom; and as a final retort, spit in Gods face, fully aware. At this point, the rock, "cut not by human hands" strikes the statue, to complete the process [Daniel 2:34] – the statue crumbles 'like chaff', and there is no longer any way to get back to the iron gates, or the beautiful gate. This is Babylon in action. Instead of shadowing Jesus, you have become like Lucifer, who left from amongst the fiery stones, The Holy Place of Heaven, and sought to overthrow God; irrevocably damned.

What strikes me about the imagery of Daniel 2:34, is that if the statue had iron legs AND feet, the rock would not have caused the statue to crumble. There is a distance one can walk away from the presence of God, even away from the faith, where, by grace, there is still hope for reconciliation. That being said, as grand as apostasy can sound, we need to realize that it is actually *relatively* easy to commit apostasy in THC. This is not a message for 'the wicked' – it is for you and for I. The crutch that you hold onto today, is precisely the thing which will instigate your irreversible descent from the presence of God, back into the bondage of hopelessness – and beyond. Babylon's covert surveillance operations were established for such a time as this; every piece of intelligence gathered, used to strike with Asp-like timing and accuracy. The Kingdom of God endows with gifts to edify and mobilize, and so recognize that the golden crutch was a custom-made gift from Babylon's gates, to keep you bound, weak and immobilized. There are individuals right now; even in leadership, who love God, who serve God, yet serve their flesh to an equal or greater measure. Schematically, these individuals <u>have left the temple</u>. Is this you? As the old adage says; a journey begins with a single step, and truly; these individuals are one step closer to committing apostasy than if they had 'stayed on the holy hill'. Committing apostasy is not as hard as the enemy would seduce you into thinking – consider Adam who walked with God in the cool of the day, yet when faced with his sin, allowed himself to be seduced out of paradise.

Everyone has a 'reasonable excuse' for not being an <u>EXACT</u> replication of what and who scripture says we are to be – but who glories in mediocrity? What is its use? What is the point of salt, if it has lost its savor, only to be trampled underfoot, or if the city set upon a hill, negates the opportunity afforded by its location and hides its lights? The revelation of God tells us that His strength is made perfect in our infirmities; not that we should continue with our reasonable excuses, but that we should assimilate, taking on His strength, reinforcing every weak place; His light illuminating our paths and providing a lamp unto our feet, toward an expected, more perfect end.

> Awake, awake; put on thy strength, O Zion; put on thy beautiful garments, O Jerusalem, the holy city: for henceforth there shall no more come into thee the uncircumcised and the unclean.
>
> -Isaiah 52:1

This is to encourage you, that regardless of what your brother and sister in Christ may or may not be doing; regardless of every single example you have seen or heard in the past; regardless of every sermon you have ever heard, which gave you permission to struggle, or contend, or make do with *unchangeable circumstances* until Jesus comes – please hear me; there is no name, no addiction, no sickness, no perversion, no appetite, no mindset, no craving and no desire known or unknown, which does not have to bow to the name of Jesus. Let us meditate on that truth – nothing else expressed from the mouth of man should ever be allowed audience in the chambers of your heart. Ultimately, Jesus is the only standard – not Moses, not David, not Solomon, not Elijah, not Paul – not even your Pastor or leader. We worship in The Kingdom of God – this is not a democracy. You are fearfully and wonderfully created and made, NOT for mediocrity, but as a triumph and a testimony. Remember love.

> **11** For I know the thoughts *and* plans that I have for you, says the Lord, thoughts *and* plans for welfare *and* peace and not for evil, to give you hope in your final outcome. **12** Then you will call upon Me, and you will come and pray to Me, and I will hear *and* heed you. **13** Then you will seek Me, inquire for, *and* require Me [as a vital necessity] and find Me when you search for Me with all your heart.
> **Jeremiah 29:11-13**
> [AMP]

CHAPTER 10

THANK YOU – THE GRATEFUL RECIPIENT (DOXOLOGY)

Is there no balm in Gilead? Is there no physician there? Why then
has not the health of the daughter of my people been restored?

Jeremiah 8:22

[KJV]

We have eaten, and we have been satisfied – how now do we apply this word, safeguarding inevitable change? How do we, in a show of gratitude not waste this food, but ensure that every mouthful is appreciated, savored, digested and utilized? How do we <u>engage</u> a seasoned, cultivated and a conditioned heart, <u>at all times</u>, so that everywhere we go, compassion can be poured liberally; heaven's rich, sweet nectar, on earth. I pray that you would continue to ruminate upon these words in your heart, and through The Holy Spirit, discern their relevant application in your life.

The term Doxology is an old word used with decreasing prevalence in the modern Christian vernacular. Its meaning is derived from two Greek words: *doxa* meaning glory, and *lagas* meaning *a word*; *to say*; or *a saying*. It is literally a 'telling forth' of God's Glory. In this respect, it is considered a high offering of thanksgiving and praise.

For astute Christians, it is our hope that our lives will become a literal, living doxology – a life which boldly speaks of and reflects God's glory, plainly and unapologetically for all to see.

FOCUS

²But as for me, my feet were almost gone; My steps had well nigh slipped. ³For I was envious at the arrogant, When I saw the prosperity of the wicked. ⁴For there are no pangs in their death; But their strength is firm. ⁵They are not in trouble as other men; Neither are they plagued like other men. ⁶Therefore pride is as a chain about their neck; Violence covereth them as a garment. ⁷Their eyes stand out with fatness: They have more than heart could wish.

Psalm 73:2-7
[ASV]

In Psalm 73, Asaph speaks very candidly of a reality which is all too familiar to most of us; as he ponders the question, 'why do the wicked prosper?' Asaph says 'my feet nearly gave way – I almost slipped when I saw (looked upon/ considered) the prosperity of the wicked; and truly, when we consider how those outside of The Kingdom have prospered, many of us would question the justice in what we see, or even slip and return to the world. There are people I went to school with – even family members, who have chosen to take that route – these are individuals who right now in all honesty, *appear* to be living a blessed life: they are healthy, solvent, most of them are in stable relationships, have healthy children, and have amassed enough so that there is an inheritance which could span more than one generation. These individuals live in a kingdom in which the laws of sickness, poverty etc., seem to have been suspended, and instead, favor washes them anew every morning. The reality is, The Bible tells us about the *wicked*, but more importantly, it tells us about the just, and how the just live – we already have a word, and so why are we concerned with the apparent prosperity of the *wicked*?

Asaph's real issue was not the wicked, or their prosperity, but the fact that he *considered* the wicked and their prosperity in the first place, and in doing so opened himself up to jealousy, envy and inevitably, insecurity – remember Lot's wife!. We need to learn to close ourselves to information that doesn't concern us! The Bible says in Philippians 4:8, '*...whatsoever things are **true**, whatsoever things are **honest**, whatsoever things are **just**, whatsoever things are **pure**, whatsoever things are **lovely**, whatsoever things are **of good report**; if there be any **virtue**, and if there be any **praise**, <u>think on these things</u>.*' Jesus said 'I AM the way, the truth, and the light' [John 14:6], and so if we are concerned with thinking on, or focusing on truth, we don't look to what we see, but to the infallible promise of God, through the eyes of faith. Asaph starts Psalm 73 with, '*Truly God is good to Israel, even to such as are of a clean heart.*' This meditation was true, honest, just, pure, lovely, of good report, virtuous, *and* there was praise within it. He had no reason to move from this meditation, and he plainly states that in doing so, it affected him negatively. When you begin to meditate upon the wicked, or on their success, you incubate this thought in your heart, when it is God's word you should have kept in your heart, with all diligence; meditating upon it day and night. Want to change what you see in your life? Lift your eyes to a higher place. If we are *waiting* on God's promises and prophetic words to manifest, meditate on these things. What I'm describing is not blind ignorance, a 'rose tinted' perspective, denial, or a technique of evasion; but a conscious decision to acknowledge what we see, <u>yet have a firm grasp on the **truth**</u>. You cannot do this on an empty stomach – you need some Word in you. The wicked *will* prosper – but we know their end, and if we have focused on what is true, as opposed to what is evident at any given time, the word says that that these same wicked people are prospered so that their wealth can be laid up for YOU AND I [Proverbs 13:22].

Interestingly, Psalm 73 is the testimony of a man who had concerned himself with the wicked, but Psalm 37 opens by saying: *Fret not thyself because of evildoers, neither be thou envious against the workers of iniquity.* In fretting ourselves over evildoers, or being envious against the workers of iniquity, we have literally <u>inverted</u> God's will for us, focusing instead on what is **false** and **deceptive**, the **unjust** and **corrupt**, **disagreeable** and **of bad report**, **immoral**, and where there be **lamentation**. Without faith, it is impossible to please God [Hebrews 11:6], and the truth is; when there is a word from God sent out that it is going to rain, people of faith don't focus on the fact that it is 100°F, and has been for the past 2 months – they are more concerned with making sure they have containers ready to receive the rain that they KNOW, in spite of how it looks, is about to fall. If you are a person who finds themselves in that place, questioning God as to why you do everything right and still struggle to get by, yet your neighbor who does everything but right, is seemingly in a better position than you, then you need to un-warp your thinking. Recognize that every time you do this, you are actually poisoning yourself, suffocating your faith, and postponing destiny. Next time you see the wicked prosper, search His Word, (which should be laid up in abundance, in your heart) for what you need, and meditate upon that; such as celebrating the blessings of Deuteronomy 28, <u>which through Christ, are all yours</u>. When the enemy comes in (even through renegade thoughts), allow the *Nahar* (flood) of God to saturate you, reminding you of who and <u>Whose</u> you are.

Although his name may not be one of the most recognizable, Asaph actually wrote a substantial portion of The Old Testament – not exclusively Psalms. Throughout the scripture, there is a very detailed picture painted of his life. Asaph was a priest from the tribe of Levi, a seer, and an individual who is noted to be a gifted musician, singer and poet. His father was Berekiah, the doorkeeper of the Ark of the Covenant. It was through his father's occupation, that a young Asaph was spotted by David, who appointed him as the musician who *played before the Ark.* Asaph became David's music director at his tent meets, and when David passed away, Asaph continued his role under Solomon in his temple. During Solomon's reign, Asaph was extremely vocal about Solomon's wickedness, making note of the fact that Solomon had put God aside, in pursuit of worldly 'wisdom', wealth, luxury, strange women and other god's. Asaph also criticized Solomon for the subsequent slavery and extortionate taxes, which he enforced to support his lavish tastes. Both Asaph and his brother Zecheriah were outspoken on the matter, and it is speculated that this in turn led to Solomon ordering Zecheriah's assassination in the temple, as referenced by Jesus in Matthew 23:35. Asaph was by all means a man of God, with a generational legacy – his father stood outside The Most Holy Place and guarded The Ark – *The Presence of God*, but during his lifetime, Asaph was actually allowed to enter in. Asaph was not a 'Johnny come lately', and although he had his own set of 'reasonable excuses', to be frank, he should have known better than to become (un)stuck on 'meaningless consideration'. Asaph, with all of his knowledge, moral uprightness, his Gifts and years spent before the presence of God, almost allowed a fleeting consideration, and the subsequent emotions of jealousy and envy to consume and destabilize him.

Asaph reminds us that a lack of focus, even fleeting, can displace a child of God – this is essentially a resurgence of *The Golden Crutch*, in that The Word of God undergirds and orders our steps – we walk by faith, not by sight, and this same faith commeth by inclining our ear to Jesus; the Word of God. The only time when a child of God loses their footing is when they choose to replace the infallible strength of Jesus, the 'solid rock', with something else.

Brethren, let us <u>reign in our focus</u>, and being of sound mind and stoic assurance; belligerently, and unwaveringly continue on, pressing toward the mark for the prize of the high calling of God in Christ Jesus.

> 'Finally, brethren, whatsoever things are true, whatsoever things are honest, whatsoever things are just, whatsoever things are pure, whatsoever things are lovely, whatsoever things are of good report; if there be any virtue, and if there be any praise, think on these things.'
> **Philippians 4:8**

MAY THE LORD MAKE US TRULY THANKFUL

Verily I say unto you, Whosoever shall not receive The Kingdom
of God as a little child, he shall not enter therein.
Mark 10:5

As a child of The New Covenant, God has laid countless promises at
your feet – there is a new paradigm of entitlement and worthiness,
through Christ, which somehow hasn't quite ministered to the
understanding of most believers. This is unfortunate, because it is
extremely important to know, and be assured in your identity, as
a child of The King. Who are you? What do you stand for? What
stands for you? How? When? WHY? We have all heard the much
hackneyed phrase before, "taking back what the enemy has stolen
from you", but if you knew who you were, in Christ, 'the enemy'
would not have even dared to touch any of your stuff in the first
place. In fact, in most instances it wasn't even taken, but you gave it
willingly because you didn't realize the true value of what you were
giving away – let's be honest. More importantly, if we don't first
understand, and then receive what has been apportioned to us, we
can never truly be thankful, and so our ignorance is a grave show of
ungrateful behavior.

Being born again, you literally become a child, in a new family.
Imagine the scenario for a second – you are born into an incredibly
rich family – a family who want for nothing. As a baby, you are
offered nutrient dense milk from the breast, but turn it down,
'*humbly*' requesting water instead, or as a toddler when given a
birthday present, you hand it back to your parents, insisting that
they should do something better with the money, or as an adolescent,
you refuse to sleep in the palatial bedroom provided for your use,
instead insisting that you want to sleep outside… this would be
ridiculous, and truly, no child would do it. Not only would it be
illogical, but to refuse something which your parents worked hard to

provide for you, even under the guise of being *'humble'*, is one of the most disrespectful things you could ever do, and is the farthest thing away from being a grateful recipient. Your place in The Kingdom of God was bought at a price – the ultimate price, and so for any of us to nonchalantly gloss over 'Kingdom acceptance' is a grave insult to Christ's legacy. The trust fund child, who sleeps rough on the street, not only spits in the face of their provision, but also presents a false image to the world about his parents and all they have done for him. Every time we stand out of line with, and at odds to scriptural promise, we do the same.

At some point in life, we learn to be 'polite' and we become schooled in the system of customary sensibilities, and public niceties. This false balance will eventually work its way into the heart, and manifests itself as an aspect of THC. Scenario: you go to an associates house, and the associate doesn't really want to go all the way to the kitchen, yet offers you a drink (in and of itself an example of THC). You know the offer is only customary, and so even though you are thirsty, you decline, stating that you just had something to drink. Not only are you supporting their THC by not calling their bluff, but you lied, displacing truth in honor of this false system. This same customary behavior is repeated time and again, in many different scenarios, and it is only a matter of time before, your **heart** will become **conditioned** toward not being able to receive, and a complex of unworthiness. When we now come into the knowledge of Christ and learn about His Kingdom, though in our head we can grasp what is being offered, and we desire it, our heart poorly modulates and through that same process of customary niceties, rejects The Kingdom.

Children do not have this issue. If a two year old is hungry, or thirsty, or 'needs potty', the child has not yet become 'refined' in the way of customary sensibilities, and so not only will this child request help, but he or she will gratefully receive any assistance offered. For this same reason, when a child is older, we teach them about 'stranger danger', which is unfortunate because as much as this is necessary within the present society, instances like that are exactly the kind of teachings which lay the framework for not being able to receive in adulthood.

> the LORD God is a sun and shield: the LORD
> will give grace and glory: no good thing will he
> withhold from them that walk uprightly.
>
> -Psalm 84:11

> I am the vine, ye are the branches: He that abideth
> in me, and I in him, the same beareth much fruit:
> for apart from me ye can do nothing.
>
> John 15:5

> And whatsoever ye shall ask in my name,
> that will I do, that the Father may be glorified in the Son.
>
> John 14:13

If any man is in Christ (who makes us righteous), and if Christ be in that individual (which makes us upright), and they have not recognized the above scriptures to be true in their personal life - God has not changed his word - and so there is a recognition that the individual has NOT received The Kingdom, as a child. Remember the heart is a modulator – like a thermostat. You could turn your heating up to 500°, but if your thermostat is set to 20°, <u>it will override your decision</u>. No matter how earnestly you desire to accept The Kingdom; if THC labors your heart, there is going to be an issue. God is not a man that He should lie, and so when He, out of His infinite resource, generosity and love extends The Kingdom to you, He doesn't require your nice, customary response. Unless you are able to address your THC, and 'reset the thermostat' to receive The Kingdom, like a little child, you will continue to push away, *by proxy*, every good thing which God has already given, in love.

Lord, teach us to receive, with a grateful heart.

Under the Table Theology

The other side of this issue is that many will never truly experience sonship, because 2,000 years after Christ, they still act as foreigners; glad to eat the crumbs from under the table when, through Christ, we have been afforded a seat at The Father's banquet. *This people draweth nigh unto me with their mouth, and honoureth me with their lips; but their heart is far from me* [Matthew 15:8]. God calls us to relationship, to sonship, which we agree to with our mouths, but out of the abundance of our heart we have indefinitely locked God into the 'kind stranger' zone, and so can only relate on this basis.

This is something I saw a lot of in my grandmother's generation; which most look to as 'the Golden generation of faithful saints', but they too had their own set of issues, which we cannot let *nostalgic romanticism* blind us to. One of the things my grandmother's generation were prone to doing, in their prayers was to cry out to God for mercy – literally, and sometimes to the point of exhaustion. The issue with this, is that grace and mercy <u>have already been given</u> – sufficiently and in abundance, through Christ, so if you are crying out for mercy, it is a clear indication toward the deficit in your comprehension of exactly what God has set on the table before you – possibly because you are *under* the table waiting for the 'kind stranger' to drop some crumbs. This is the *Under the Table Theology*. You cannot beg for something you already have. The appropriate response is therefore thanksgiving. However, understand that even the act of mindless thanksgiving can too expose an individual who does not view themselves as a worthy son, through Christ, and therefore not only negates the privileges of this relationship, but also denies Christ and His ability as an all sufficient atonement, every time they operate from a place of unworthiness.

*Speaking and living out the truth of who God says you are, is the **purest** form of humility an individual could ever express.*
-Min. James Francis, UK

Through Christ we are worthy partakers of all the good gifts of heaven. Someone pays $2,000 for a ticket to an exclusive banquet for you, and you turn up, thank the individual unreservedly, yet stay outside to show how much you revere the gift – it's nonsensical, as well as being an insult to the individual who bought (at a great price) your ticket. The only true show of thanks and gratitude would be for you to turn up, to enter in, and receive all which that *expensive ticket* entitles you to - the only desire of the individual who purchased it for you in the first place. It's truly the posturing of the heart which defines the difference between thanksgiving and the debased interpretation of thanksgiving, which is an insult to God.

Imagine you adopt a baby – you obviously want that baby to be acclimatized to being a part of your family. However if from baby to toddler, toddler to child, child to pre-pubescent, pre-pubescent to adolescent…. that individual does not grasp the concept of *vicarious consanguinity*, or the entitlement which comes from being a part of a family, so that every time you feed the child, the child thanks you in the way of a lodger, or buy clothes for the child, the child thanks you in the way of a homeless person receiving alms - understand that this causes a rift in the relationship. As a man thinketh in his heart, so is he. If you have been declared as a son, yet in your heart, you see yourself as an unworthy sinner, you push the provision of salvation [sozo] away by considering yourself, in your heart, less than what God Almighty declares you to be. God did not exalt us to the rank of a joint heir with Christ, only for us to find our way back to the dirt in 'humility' and grovel in a strange show of thanks to our own Father. This is in fact the greatest show of ingratitude. God has invited us into the paradigm of relationship, but many of us have not let go of the old paradigm of unknown foreigner. In doing so, we throw God's extension of love back in His face, and being a 'gentleman'; God will never force you to be or do something you have so plainly displayed you have no intention being or doing. We need to check the condition of our hearts.

When we make supplication for something we already have – such as forgiveness, we pray amiss and frustrate The Holy Spirit. This is akin to vain, meaningless repetition: chanting, like the 'heathen' – those without the knowledge of Christ [Matt. 6:7]. We cannot pray for Jesus to be crucified again, but we can thank God for Calvary, and the all-sufficient forgiveness it has already afforded. This is what a grateful recipient does! If we cannot receive what is already in front of us, then what is the point of giving us anything else? *Holy Spirit, help us to cultivate a heart, receptive to you, and all that you have laid before us.*

Neither should we vainly chant our thanks in some strange offering to 'appease' God. The truth is, you could never adequately thank God, and so He has released us from this burden – for all that He has done, ALL He wants in return is our hearts. God is not slack concerning His promises [2 Peter 3:9], and so the individual who reacts in shock, surprise, disbelief and unworthiness when God performs that which was promised, exposes their level of relationship with this 'benevolent stranger'. Thanksgiving without understanding is a way we frequently do this.

Lord, teach us to cultivate a heart-understanding of relationship, and open our eyes to see, understand and receive the spread, which you, in your infinite love toward us have laid out before us. For this, and for an innumerable plethora of blessings; for what you have set before us to receive, may The Lord make us TRULY thankful. AMEN.

THE BALM

Out of the abundance of the heart, flow the issues of life - we are in fact a manifestation of our hearts. Please take a moment to reflect upon and consider the truth of that statement. This is why THC is such a problem.

In the first chapter, we briefly touched on the topic of heaven; the dwelling place of God, and how in allowing God to dwell in our hearts, we have allowed heaven to be ordered; The Kingdom of Heaven within, as referred to by Jesus [Luke 17:21]. As carriers of 'heaven' i.e. those who have chosen to keep righteousness in their hearts, God plants us in the land.

> [39] And I will give them one heart, and one way, that they may fear me for ever, for the good of them, and of their children after them. [41] Yea, I will rejoice over them to do them good, and I will plant them in this land assuredly with my whole heart and with my whole soul
> **Jeremiah 32:39+41**
> [KJV]

In doing so, not only have we planted heaven through our lifestyle of compassion, but God has planted us – remember we are a manifestation of our hearts, and so by planting us in the land, God Himself has planted heaven. This is why the earth groans and travails with labour pains [Romans 8] – in anticipation for 'the revelation of the Sons of God' - the harvest; when that which God has hidden and planted in the land bursts forth and can be reaped and enjoyed: heaven on earth.

Jeremiah 8:22 poses the rhetorical question: Is there no balm in Gilead? Is there no physician there? Clearly the problem is not the lack of balm, nor the lack of a physician, as the verse continues; ..."Why then has not the health of the daughter of my people been restored?" When we think on how many churches there are at this hour; even mega-churches, how many teachers, prophets, apostles evangelists and pastors– how many Christians period, it should tear our heart apart to recognise that although yes – we hold the balm, and yes – we have direct access to the physician, there is yet so much hurt, pain and confusion upon the face of the planet. So much avoidable, unnecessary suffering. It is exciting to know that we are carriers of heaven, and that *the Kabod* of God dwells within it, but to what gain? Truly what is the point of being salt, if we have lost our savour? What is the point if a city set upon a hill has no visible light, and hides its true beauty? What is the point of a church building, if all it provides is a weekly babysitting service for grown adults who really should know better? Truly, we have lost the plot somewhere along the line, and with it, the ability to comprehend through our hearts; the heart of Christ.

Every day, we are walking in the unveiling of Biblical prophecy, and just like in the days of Noah, when people were 'marrying and being given in marriage', month on month, the level of depravity in *acceptable society* waxes worse. There is such a thick level of deception upon the earth at this time; so many demonic, anti-Christ agendas being pushed; and subsequently, so many who are disenfranchised, angry, hurt and confused. The pain upon the face of this earth right now is immense, and every night as we close our eyes to sleep, many will cry tears of desperation; tears sowed in vain, ignorant of the fact that only Jesus can stem the flow - replacing their melancholy with true, tangible joy. Every individual upon the face of the planet has been given a heart, and the hurt, fear, pain and disorientation will continue, until these individuals are brought to the realisation that there is no suitable alternative to be found, which can fill that 'God-shaped hole', save God Himself.

We know that it will yet be a little while before this whole system is bought to its knees. However, at such a time as this, we are not called to be passive spectators, but to whom much has been given, much is expected – there is MUCH to be accomplished in the meantime. It is a shocking unjust balance for us to hold so much power, so much set before us; yet we stand powerless like Lot's wife, in empathy, but with no movement, no work, and in doing so we cast our worship to the ground. We say we represent love, but where is the proof when there are people in our sphere of influence who have never heard about the sozo of Jesus Christ, and have lost hope. WHERE IS the balm of Gilead?

There are many good works being done by Christians, Christian organisations and churches worldwide – at the level of empathy, i.e.: there is only so much your money and good intentions can accomplish. Money will allow you to build an infrastructure on rotten foundations, but when you act out of compassion, truly the heart of God builds the entire vision from the foundations up, and sets a new mind in the people.

> *"Give a man a fish and you feed him for a day;*
> *teach a man to fish and you empower him to feed*
> *his entire family for generations to come."*

What did Jesus do? Jesus went around not building edifices in His name, but Jesus established The Kingdom, by being <u>moved, in power</u>, through compassion, everywhere He went: transforming lives in a way that no amount of good intention or money ever could. Please do not misunderstand - money is important, and a lot of good work can be done with it, but the establishment of real change is only observed when an obedient vessel is willing to yield their heart to The Father, and <u>do the work</u> of reinforcing the will of God on earth; 'planting heaven', one seed at a time.

Whenever we hear of a tragedy on the news, a natural disaster, it is the easiest thing for our heart to go out to those people and for us to start arranging monies toward the cause, but STOP... What is God saying? What would the Heart of God have you do? Yes, after a natural disaster people need to rebuild their lives, and there is definitely a ministry in Christians being noticed as 'early responders', but how would God have you minister and effectively bring change to those people's lives. **How are you going to teach them to fish?** The truth is, a disenfranchised person would say yes to anything and anyone that would come along and give their lives a bit of stability. Does that mean they have experienced any level of deep revelation concerning Christ and His sozo? No. Images of a mother in tears of joy as missionaries hand out food parcels, are similarly genuine indicators of gratefulness, but does this signify that sozo has been established in this mother, and her child(ren)'s lives? NO. Of course, this work is good, but we The Kingdom, have been summoned to a far greater calling. It is through compassion that these individuals will receive an encounter with God, impacting their lives so profoundly that it would change them forever, thus establishing Christ's Kingdom on earth.

It is important to grasp this, because in the times we now live, there are personal situations so complex that there is no amount of finance, human wisdom, intellect, experience or understanding which could effectively negotiate true acceptance and assimilation of Christ into that individual's life. For example, there are individuals who have, in their lost state, mutilated their bodies to such a degree that they are virtually unrecognisable as human – case in point, the (late) 'stalking cat', aka Dennis Avner: an individual who had multiple surgeries to transform his appearance from human man, to that of a female cat. In the latter part of his life this man lived in Nevada – a state where there are many Christians who would have been equipped to minister the sozo of Christ to this clearly unhappy man, but no one was able to efficaciously move in compassion, in a way that impacted and changed his life forever (if any even attempted). In 2012 'stalking cat' was found dead in his garage after committing suicide. Which of you can minister peace to this broken man's heart now? The same is true of the late Amy Winehouse – I live in London, and I know a handful of Christians who had personal access to Ms. Winehouse, but again; <u>where was the balm of Gilead?</u> It is not enough to just get to the door, but through compassion <u>we need to enter in</u>, and effect change. However knowing that this is the same heart condition which causes Christians to stay outside the doors to The Kingdom and not enter in, it stands to reason. <u>We need to check the condition of our hearts.</u>

Truly, where is the balm, which can be applied to the mentality, multiple psychoses and the physical, spiritual and emotional scarring of an individual who has undergone gender reassignment surgery - whilst in love, effectually ministering healing to the WHOLE person? How do we, as a body, receive this person; safeguarding their decision to accept Christ? This is the stark, light-of-day reality of the world in which we live today. <u>Yet the ability of God to minister to a heart,</u>

and Calvary to save, heal and deliver is unchanged. Brethren, there is MUCH work to be done.

COMPLACENCY

As individuals under the new covenant, complacency is something that we need to put to bed, daily. The issue is that it has so many different manifestations, all bearing a different image. At one end of the scale you have the individuals who live exactly the same sinful life they lived before they accepted Christ, charging it to 'grace', and then you have the more subtle manifestations of complacency, like the sudden irrational flare-up of anger which we didn't know was there, or the unexpected lie we so readily told when in a tight spot. All complacency is bad, but subtle is worse, because it is hidden and the individual has no idea they have been complacent/ taken their eye off the ball until something strange and unexpected manifests; thus exposing said complacency. Complacency is a heart condition in which the heart hardens itself to something which it perceives it already knows. Imagine sitting in Bible study, and the moderator asks everyone to tell the group their favorite scripture, and explain how it has impacted their life. One individual stands and says John 3:16 - for God so loved the world, that He gave His only begotten Son... As Christians, we know this scripture 'by heart', and so there is an opportunity for complacency to slip in, under the assumption that 'there's nothing new I can learn from that... I already know the meaning of that scripture... NEXT!" The complacent heart is a dangerous thing and will cause us to have surface revelation, surface relationships, and to live a surface reality; comprehending sweetness, but never really 'tasting the honey'.

Some time ago, God revealed this very issue to me in a dream:

I was at my mother's house, and I had made a meal for my family. Everyone had eaten, and my brother asked me for a second helping of fish. Now bear in mind that this fish was already cooked, and so it only needed a few minutes heating, but I found myself in the kitchen 'browning' the fish in a frying pan, to the point that after some minutes, I moved the fish onto a huge floor griddle-like contraption, which must have been about 3m^2 in size. As I went to turn the fish, I realized that I was actually dealing with chicken, and that some of the pieces were still undercooked on one side. So I continued to cook the chicken, turning regularly to avoid burning. During this process, turning each piece of meat, to my surprise, I suddenly realized that there was also a whole fox mixed in with the pieces of meat, which looked as though it had been cooked on a griddle, flattened out fillet style – weird, yes, but from fish to chicken, from chicken to fox.. within the ambit of the dream, it wasn't as alarming as it would be in real life. I turned up the heat, and left the pieces of chicken, and the fox for a few minutes to brown off – the skin was beginning to caramelize, and from the rich aroma that was now filling the kitchen, I could tell that it was almost done. When I came back, the fox, which was almost ready for consumption just moments prior, was now up, walking about, on the griddle! Our eyes met, and it looked as shocked as I was. I paced toward it, and it ran off. This dream was very profound, and even as I recall it now, the memory is just as vivid. When I woke up, The Holy Spirit began to give me interpretation, which continued throughout that day.

The imagery of the flesh in this dream referred to 'blind spots'. These aren't limited to the flesh, but could also be something within the spirit or the soul, which you have neglected to notice and take appropriate action over. For clarity, every time I refer to the *flesh from* here onward, I am referring to any unruly area(s) within the whole being, whether located in the spirit, soul, body or indeed heart. For many of us, as far as we are concerned, we have laid our *flesh* on the altar, and it has been conformed to the will of God – the fish has been cooked to such a level, that even your own brother will confirm how well seasoned you have become…

When our platform changes, or we have a change of circumstances, opportunity arises to gain an insight into our *flesh* that we didn't have before. I thought it was fish, and so did everyone else, but it turned out to be chicken. It's only now when you look at this *flesh* with new eyes that you recognize that not only is the *flesh* not what you initially thought it was, but the *flesh* has not even been fully conformed to God – it's still partially raw! Suddenly there is a fox in the mix – this should have freaked me out, but I carried on cooking regardless. In complacency there are some seriously obvious things that we choose to turn a blind eye to, because we are so assured within ourselves. In reality I should have at least investigated/ questioned why despite not cooking fox, there was fox on the griddle. Symbolically, a fox is an unclean beast in the OT law: a member of the dog family, and so represents lusts, hedonism and the various displays of an insatiable appetite, whether manifested out of the soul, body or spirit. It can also speak of a wayward heart. Biblically dogs can also represent demonic messengers, or a demonic decree. A fox is not only a dog, but a very intelligent dog – remember the phrase; as cunning as a fox? This is essentially identical to 'Babylon', with its many manifestations, but one parent spirit. We cannot afford to be complacent as children of God, but must diligently continue the conditioning process of returning our hearts to God. DAILY.

Just before the fox got up, I **smelled** that the meat was done. My **discernment** of the situation was off! It is so easy to spot the speck in another's eye, but we are most often unable to discern the plank in our own. Thankfully toward the end of the dream, I chased the fox away - but the reality is, many of us don't, and had the fox remained on the griddle with all the cooked meat, understand that the fox (the unclean thing) would consume the chicken and the fish (the clean thing, which has been subjected to the fire). Eventually all that would be left would be the unclean thing... fat, healthy and thriving.

It isn't enough to just kill certain issues - there comes a time when we have to remove the accursed thing [Joshua 7:13]. Usually, this is nigh on impossible; like the parable of the tares and the wheat in Matthew, because the two types flesh are indistinguishable. However, The Bible says *"For the word of God is quick, and powerful, and sharper than any two-edged sword, piercing even to the dividing asunder of soul and spirit, and of the joints and marrow, and is a discerner of the thoughts and intents of the heart".* [Heb. 4:12]. The word of God is a capable surgeon with the ability to navigate the subtle nuances of flesh, and remove the superfluous, inexorable pieces, with precision.

Have you ever noticed how children are completely satisfied reading the same bedtime story night after night, after night? This is not due to them being unintelligent, or having forgotten, because as I'm sure you have experienced in some way shape or form, even children who can't read will still be able to recall, verbatim, the entire story from cover to cover. These children are yet able to find joy and new depth in the story they have read twenty times in as many nights – their minds are eager to build the fullness of the whole picture, in vivid color, and their hearts have not yet been conditioned into the arrogance of complacency.

> *Father – I'm willing, and my heart is open to You like never before. I come to You as a child – as fresh clay on the wheel; malleable, ductile and ready to be molded. Soften my heart toward You; show me how to cultivate a heart whose condition Is conducive to deeper relationship in every aspect of my life, 24/7, and teach me how to diligently KEEP this heart with absolute integrity in all that I think, say and do(n't). In accordance with Your Word, and to Your eternal glory I pray. Amen.*

If you feel that after reading this book, you need to have some conversations with friends or family members, settle some grievances, or to take some time out of ministry to regroup, I would encourage you to do so. To reiterate the point made in the first chapter – this is only a book. There is no glory in you reading *The Heart Condition* – this has merely been a series of conversations; a catalogue for change. The glory comes from the conscious decision to have those conversations with The Holy Spirit, choosing to apply the revelation of those conversations and 'working out the kinks', leaning on Jesus' strength toward an expected end. There is nothing stagnant about this walk, and His will is to stabilize you from faith to faith, from glory to glory. Today, make the decision to truly work out your own salvation, loving God with ALL of your heart, soul, strength and mind.

In closing, be encouraged that God's work in you is not yet finished, and that if you would actively seek to condition your heart; becoming sensitive to Him in every area of your life, line by line and precept upon precept; you would see God's transformative power move in your life <u>like never before.</u>

> [19] [That you may really come] to know [practically, through experience for yourselves] the love of Christ, which far surpasses mere knowledge [without experience]; that you may be filled [through all your being] unto all the fullness of God [may have the richest measure of the divine Presence, and become a body wholly filled and flooded with God Himself]!
> **Ephesians 3:19**
> [AMP]

But it is The God of grace who has called us to His eternal glory by Jesus The Christ, who gives us, while we shall endure these small afflictions, to yet be empowered, confirmed and established in Him; even until eternity.

1 Peter 5:10
[Aramaic Bible in Plain English]

Lightning Source UK Ltd.
Milton Keynes UK
UKOW04f0851100216

268041UK00001B/8/P